Quintessence Series

Series editor

Nils Bickhoff
Quintessential Strategies
Hamburg, Germany

More information about this series at http://www.springer.com/series/10376

Stefan Hase • Corinna Busch

The Quintessence of Sales

What You Really Need to Know
to Be Successful in Sales

 Springer

Stefan Hase
Wirkung Plus GmbH
Hamburg, Germany

Corinna Busch
Wirkung Plus GmbH
Hamburg, Germany

ISSN 2195-4941   ISSN 2195-495X   (electronic)
Quintessence Series
ISBN 978-3-319-61172-3   ISBN 978-3-319-61174-7   (eBook)
DOI 10.1007/978-3-319-61174-7

Library of Congress Control Number: 2017946181

Cover design: eStudio Calamar, Berlin/Figueres

Printed on acid-free paper

This Springer imprint is published by Springer Nature
The registered company is Springer International Publishing AG
The registered company address is: Gewerbestrasse 11, 6330 Cham, Switzerland

We thank Frank Sandtmann for his constructive comments and valuable suggestions on this book. Frank, you rock!

Contents

List of Figures

List of Tables

Sales is no rocket science. As we started working on this book 2 years ago, a good friend—and experienced business analyst—did a research for us on the existing literature status. His feedback was "Amazing, how low the written level in sales is compared to other areas like marketing or psychology. There are a lot of no-brainers such as 'work more,' 'do more calls,' or 'get up more early.' Is this really all, what sales is about?"

The answer is: Yes and No. Yes, the existing approaches about sales are indeed often pretty fragmented and superficial. There are some really good books, but mainly they are about the micro-perspective. Meaning: "How to... e.g. win more customers—gain more margin...." But focusing only on these (in fact: very important) skill factors, one ignores the at least equally important macro aspect of sales. So, No, this isn't the entire story. There is much more to explore. There is also a demanding organizational framework to establish against a lot of political resistance, and to "free" sales from this unit thinking, and establish it as the accepted driver of the entire company.

What is also remarkable: Even by being called as one of the oldest professions in the world, there is hardly any accepted, established, and common education path for it. In fact, most salespeople do get a classical education in business and industry (e.g., business people, engineers, trade, banking industry, insurance,...), and then, they change their career path and switch into this completely new field of business. In their new position, they generally receive a good technical education, but just rarely run through a professional sales training program.

This leads to a very high percentage of self-taught sales reps who do their very best—in the way they have gained experience as outsiders and observers, and from their own individual practice. To rely mainly on what the company's salespeople do believe is best seems—especially in this complex business environment with its tough competition nowadays—risky and somehow outdated. Quite a lot of those people who changed to a sales career do not even name themselves "sales staff." Rather, they like to call themselves—due to their professional background—"technical experts," "supporter," or "consultant." That's something special in this

© Springer International Publishing AG 2018

S. Hase, C. Busch, *The Quintessence of Sales*, Quintessence Series,
DOI 10.1007/978-3-319-61174-7_1

twenty-first century, in which many other branches take over a more and more scientific approach. Just give it a thought, when your doctor, or banker, or lawyer or even your pilot would be mainly an autodidact and would not have a proper background education...

It's like always in life. Only if you mix your ingredients in a certain balance you achieve something special. So the task is to define for this still emerging management discipline an appropriate balance between human factor, effective structure-shaping organization and modern tools science. And beware of the following: Due to the partial absence of hard facts, soft skills are in sales the true hard skills. Does that sound promising? OK, to keep you going, we got one more! You won't find any demanding equations in this book. If you hope to see that, you should have paid more attention to advanced maths. Promise!

Having said that, we have four questions for you to check that this book will really benefit you:

1. What Is the Goal of this Book?
Our goal with this book is:

- That you have a reference book for various situations as well as a how-to manual for your practice
- That you understand the different steps of an efficient sales process to cope with the current requirements
- That you have an overview of the organizational framework required to build a sales organization
- That you can define the different kind of sales players that are involved, and know how to build a successful sales team
- That you are familiar with the most important sales management tasks and responsibilities

2. What Makes it Special?
We like to combine the micro (i.e., personal skill set and enabling) with the macro perspective (i.e., structure, organizational framework, leadership). Sales is in our opinion, and to agree with Brian Tracy (2015, p. 3), an American great, "an inexact science." But at least it is one—and it is not only a subdivision of marketing.

3. What Qualifies Us to Write this Book?
Over the last decade, we had the thankworthy opportunity to work for our customers around the globe in different economical hot spots. This includes the United States, Canada, South America, Russia, China, Asia Pacific, and many European countries. We attended a lot of real major customer meetings as we shadowed salespeople in their daily business. Therefore, we gained interesting insights at first-hand in different markets, as well as both a local and cultural understanding, and we got to know various negotiation approaches and techniques from the big players.

The second milestone is that the Europäische Fernhochschule Hamburg (Euro-FH) cooperated with us in the design and implementation of the first German bachelor degree course in "Sales Management" in 2012–2013. As a typical German course of study, this requires a proven structure on how sales is efficiently practiced today. For the last 4 years, we have now conducted over 100 sales workshops on six different major topics with over 500 ambitious attendees, which are heading out for being the sales leaders of the future. And we are happy to say: Mission accomplished.

4. Who Is the Target Group?

This book is not only for sales experts.[1] In fact, most REAL salespeople do not like to read any advisers! Why? Because they are—to quote somebody from this species—"so experienced, that we know everything already."

Besides these so-called "sales natives," we like to address all "normal" sales colleagues from all level of hierarchies: Rookies, account managers, key account managers, team leaders, sales directors, and so forth. Our aim is to give you a condensed overview and to offer guidance as well as the opportunity to double check your current approach and eventually gain some new ideas. This includes also the mentioned career changers for whom we like to establish a professional background for their new field of business.

Another target group is the management at all levels, such as owners, C-Suite members, managers, and decision makers, because they have to understand the setup of the driver of the company—which is sales—and how to implement required sales structures and to define possible shortcuts. With this knowledge, it will be easier to predict the capabilities and limitations of a professional sales organization. By the way, out of our personal experience: For our former CFO, it was not easy to understand why 30% more sales staff would not immediately result in 30% more turnover.

In addition, this book is also written for (so far) non-sales people. Whether their field of expertise is finance, HR, engineering, IT, admin, or marketing or something else: Sooner or later they will be touching the sales domain, and this book will help them to understand "terra incognita." Especially, what keeps the sales guys going, and how to establish synergies with their own area, and how to facilitate energy and straightforward attitude of the sales colleagues.

And last but not least, this book is written for all ambitious people, who are involved in boosting their career and their business, because without knowing the sales mechanisms, this will be much tougher to achieve.

How to Read this Book

This book is not necessarily written to be read in one sweep. It also functions as a reference book. Choose the topic which can help you in your daily business. In this

---

[1]For reasons of readability, only the male form is used in this book; however, the female form is also always intended.

regard, we think you agree that metaphors are useful in sales. And music and sports are real good translators. Therefore, we like to play the following "set list."

First, we like to give you a first basic understanding and set the Sales Arena. What influences the game? What are must-haves, and what are nice-to-haves? The often heard statement of natural born sales experts sounds good—but it is just a catchy line. You won't control any modern system efficiently if you do not know each single parameter.

Second, we like to illustrate the different phases of the sales process. Structure is key and will provide you with the right direction.

Third, the sales environment and the relevant sales players that are involved will be outlined. The fourth and final part of this book will be about managing and developing sales.

All our ideas will focus on the B2B level. This is the relevant champions' league, and requires in comparison to B2C a much more sophisticated approach.

Due to the scope of this book, we cannot go into all bits and bytes. Sometimes, if available, we will offer you links so that you can continue your interesting journey. Our aim is to explore the big scope of this profession.

And last but not least: Sales is supposed to be gripping and in best case emotional—otherwise you lose contact pretty quickly. Therefore, this book is written with our understanding of humor. For readers used to enjoy purely scientific stuff, this may be some challenge... But writing about a deeply human topic and ignoring one of the essential ingredients for effective communication, it would be like AC/DC with no guitar...

Reference

Tracy, B. (2015). *Sales management*. New York: American Management Association.

The Dawn of the Sales Age: A First Basic Understanding

2

Since the Lehman crisis 2008, almost everyone speaks of dynamic markets and rapid developments. What is then the actual status of sales? Has something relevant changed here in the last years?

Critics like to stress at that point that "sales has always been the same" and it is not difficult to learn it, because it either runs in your blood or not. That's a catchy line but fortunately incorrect. Counter question: Has the world favorite number one sport "soccer"—measured by the FIFA Soccer World Championship—changed since 1986? Many people think it has not: There are still 2 teams with 11 players, the game lasts for 90 min, and so on.

In fact, soccer has changed ever since. Just take a look at the—nowadays existing—numerous statistics: For example, the individual running distances per game has been extended enormously (up to 12 km for 90 min), and the role of the goalkeeper has changed. Manuel Neuer, for instance, revolutionized the position of the goalie with his proactive "playing" approach. It is a similar development within sales. Details do matter.

Let's dive into how the sales game has changed within recent years:

1. *The balance*: As customers, we (yes, you are also included) have become much more demanding and powerful. As a consequence, there is less mid- and long-term loyalty toward brands and people. The sales side has recognized this alarming trend and has shown nervous signs of response. Sad side note: In order to boost their business, the industry has made us customers much more price driven.
2. *The new role of the purchase order department (POD)*: Meanwhile, people are often chosen as buyers—and must decide over signing a contract—although they are not really familiar with the topic. This makes every sales activity, e.g., like needs assessment and argumentation, much more demanding, which is—of course—their reason for being: To achieve the best price–performance ratio for their company.

© Springer International Publishing AG 2018
S. Hase, C. Busch, *The Quintessence of Sales*, Quintessence Series,
DOI 10.1007/978-3-319-61174-7_2

3. *The complexity*: Buying and selling does not only take place between two people anymore. Other players are increasingly involved on both the customer (such as POD, finance, legal, or outsourced consultants) and the sales side (e.g., product specialists, own finance employees).

4. *The (almost threatening) transparency*: The Internet created a global village where transparency rules and where better options are just one click away. Therefore, competition is now omnipresent and every company—as technical driven as they can be—has to sell nowadays. The difference is that your competitor is now often not some regional enterprise but a global player who offers equally good products and services in your home market via the Internet.

5. *The sales pressure*: Sales teams and budget projects have no buffer. There is almost always a sales crisis! Such as in soccer: Manchester United or Real Madrid cannot lose three friendly matches without fearing that one's own job will be up for grabs.

6. *The competition*: The differentiation between your own products and services versus your competition has to be clear. There are plenty of followers with "me-too" products. This requires professional explanation of the question: What makes the key difference?

7. *The scope*: Technical-driven companies which were mainly focusing on engineering over decades now shift. The former typical mechanical engineer develops slowly into a much more communicative-driven "sales engineer." So the job scope widens significantly.

8. *The speed*: Viral marketing and the huge coverage of social and public media function as accelerators for any development. Formerly successful companies can struggle or even fail within an incredible short time frame. Vice versa, new competitors emerge barely out of nothing.

9. *Last but not least: Bad experiences*: The example of the emissions scandal in the German automobile industry visualizes unfortunately once more: Trust no one. It's often only sales talk and "too good to be true" advertising sales offers. Sad but true? Every time we become more skeptical and cautious.

The conclusion is: Never before, there has been such a huge amount of data available for the buying side, which is so easy to access and gives valid information. In order to stay competitive and earn sufficient margin, there is a strong need for every company to professionally support the selling of their products and services. After the IT age—which is still shaping the setup for economical business—the dawn of the sales age is now breaking.

2.1   The Basics in Sales

We are not totally alone. There are—as you may have noticed—many thousands of books, blogs, and advisers, telling you their approach and specific understanding about sales. Some of them even share their "secrets" and "formulas" about how to succeed. Sales has become a big "melting pot" and offers a wide variety of literature with different approaches.

What we do focus on is both a structured and holistic sales approach. In our understanding, structure is vital. And in our various trips abroad, we recognized that this typical "structured German thinking" is something absolutely valuable all over the place. Moreover, we cannot just look at single aspects of sales, such as "What makes a good salesperson or sales leader?" while blanking out everything else. There is much more to sales. Such as: How to build a winning sales team and a high-quality sales organization? And what principles of sales management do I need to apply to be readily equipped for immediate and lasting sales success?

In order to reach a common understanding and vision of sales, we will now define the sales framework and focus on some important distinctions that have to be made. It lays the foundation for the journey in the chapters that follow.

2.1.1   Definition and Core Elements of Sales

But what actually is sales? Many people think of sales as one of the 4P's of marketing: Product, price, place, and promotion. In our view, *sales* is not some sub-function of marketing but an own management discipline. Such as Zig Ziglar (2003, p. xiii), a well-known American author, puts it: "Sales is more than a profession; it's a way of life."

For us, sales is an independent, complex combination of different sciences, including psychology, communication, organization, leadership, and control. Sales is the main turnover and profit driver of any business. This is the "front line" where key business successes are prepared and put into practice. Not only future profits but also jobs and share prices are heavily dependent on sales.

The interesting about sales is:

- Many people think that they can sell—but cannot if they are viewed from outside, and be objectively measured by key performance indicators (e.g., for new customers, turnover, margin).
- Some people can sell—but do not know exactly why. If you ask them "How have you achieved this deal?," they say "I do not know—It is just the way I always do it."
- Some people can explain a lot—but fail in their execution in their daily activities to transform their knowledge into results.

There are in fact many single images of sales (i.e., acquisition, price, negotiation, customer service) but hardly a "big picture" of how everything is connected. The truth: Some facets are partially trivial and easy to manage for various types of salespersons. In a decathlon, the 100-m race will be easy for a sprinter—the discus throwing probably less.

In fact, sales is complex. *Salespeople* need many different selling skills. Such as in the decathlon, sales reps need endurance, agility, speed, and power. So everybody has to align their personal setup to required sales activities (i.e., decathlon disciplines). But that's not all. They will never be successful in sales if one essential quality is missing: A positive mindset and attitude toward the core of their business. The reason is obvious: If the attitude is negative, the salesperson sees many obstacles and takes little or no action at all. However, if the salesperson's mindset is positive, he sees opportunities and thinks the best of an idea, people, and situations. The same is central to competitive sports: The mindset decides often over win or loss.

Developing individual salespeople into a "winning sales team" is one part. The fact that better offers are only a click away has had a direct impact on marketing, distribution, and logistics processes—and as a result—on sales in general. In such keenly competitive times, another relevant task of sales managers is to (re-)shape their own *sales organization* that is inevitably oriented toward the customer. This also means the reinterpretation of traditionally "sales-averse" areas such as production, research and development, and administration. At the same time, it requires them to take control of these interfunctional interfaces and processes. In concrete terms, that means developing a holistic sales concept. This, in turn, offers many benefits such as fast market responsiveness and the creation of superior customer value by efficiently coordinating the marketing activities.

A sales organization is a reflection of its leader. Shortcomings in sales force performance can usually be traced to inadequacy in *sales management*. Hence, sales managers must be able to influence the behavior of the sales team toward the attainment of the company's objectives, goals, and values. They must also strive for developing mutually profitable long-run relationships with customers.

To put it in a nutshell, sales is the gearing of all personal activities *and* all areas of the business to the successful, high-margin selling of the company's products and services. Sales is the focal point of business management and determines the thinking and activities of an entire organization.

2.1.2 Differentiation Between B2B and B2C Selling

Salespeople and marketers often distinguish between two major categories of types of selling: Business-to-business (B2B) and business-to-consumer (B2C). As shown in Fig. 2.1, we speak of B2B markets, when it comes to business relationships between two manufacturers or the sale of products and services to wholesale or retail. By contrast, B2C refers to the market of end users.

B2C markets are markets where the distinguishing character is that the customer is purchasing products and services for their own use. Hence, the principal motives for purchase are personal in nature. There are three types of sub-markets (Jobber & Lancaster 2012):

1. *Fast-moving consumer goods (FMCG)*: FMCG markets are markets where customers purchase products, which involve relatively low financial outlays. They are bought frequently and are generally non-durable. They include

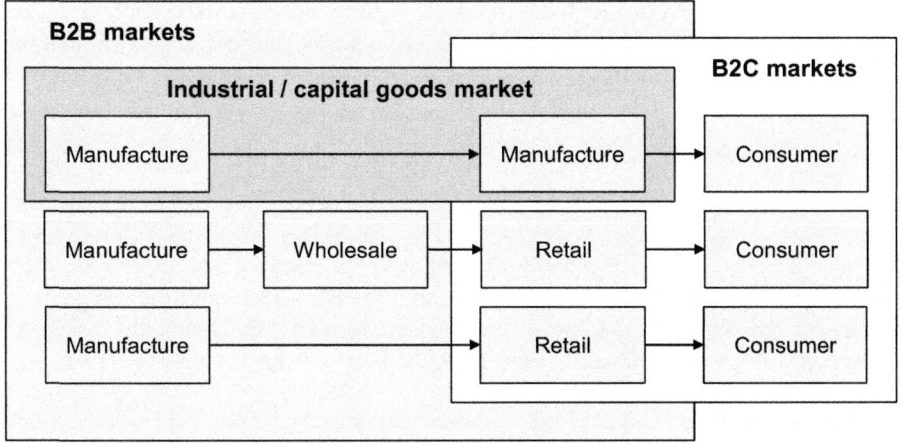

Fig. 2.1 Differentiation between B2B and B2C markets [Source: Adapted from Kreutzer, Rumler, and Wille-Baumkauff (2014, p. 13)]

products such as toothpaste, cigarettes, and grocery products. Consumers will spend relatively little time searching for information and evaluating different product offerings. If consumers are satisfied, they usually buy the same brand on a routine basis. These products are often referred to as low-involvement products.

2. *Durable consumer goods*: As the term suggests, durable consumer goods are purchases which are made less frequently. They include products such as cars, laptops, and refrigerators. Consumers often look for information and take considerable care in choosing between product offerings. This is why these products are referred to high-involvement products.

3. *Semi-durable consumer goods*: Semi-durable consumer goods include products that are bought less frequently than FMCG products and that tend to last longer. They include products such as clothing and shoes. Hence, the customer also tends to spend more time on choosing between product offerings.

B2B markets are often characterized by large and powerful buyers. These buyers purchase predominantly in an organizational context. They are much more likely to negotiate on price. This is why salespeople are likely to be dealing with highly skilled negotiators. Also the selling process may extend over months or even years for certain types of investments (e.g., new machinery for production line). As discussed by Jobber and Lancaster (2012), there are several types of sub-markets within B2B markets. These include:

• Markets for supplies and consumables (e.g., raw materials, semi-manufactured goods)
• Markets for capital equipment (e.g., machinery)
• Markets for business services (e.g., consultancy)

In this book, we lay the focus on B2B selling—due to its complexity and relevance. Once readers understand the underlying mechanisms, they can transfer the knowledge to B2C selling.

2.1.3 Factors of Modern Selling

Nowadays, selling requires a wide array of skills to compete successfully, which will be discussed later. First of all, we like to discuss six factors of modern selling which are given in Fig. 2.2 (for details, see Moncrief & Marshall 2005). If salespeople do not understand these factors, they will be ill-equipped to tackle their sales jobs. Let's have a closer look:

- *Customer relationship management (CRM)*: All activities are directed toward building *and* developing customer relationships. The emphasis should lie on creating win–win situations with customers so that both parties want to continue the relationship. This also means that sales forces should focus at least on mid term and not simply on closing a one-time sale. Ideal is, of course, the long-term focus.
- *Marketing the product*: Modern salespeople are involved in a much broader range of activities. Apart from selling—which is already challenging enough—they often also participate in strategic sales activities (e.g., product development and market development) and support sales activities (e.g., database

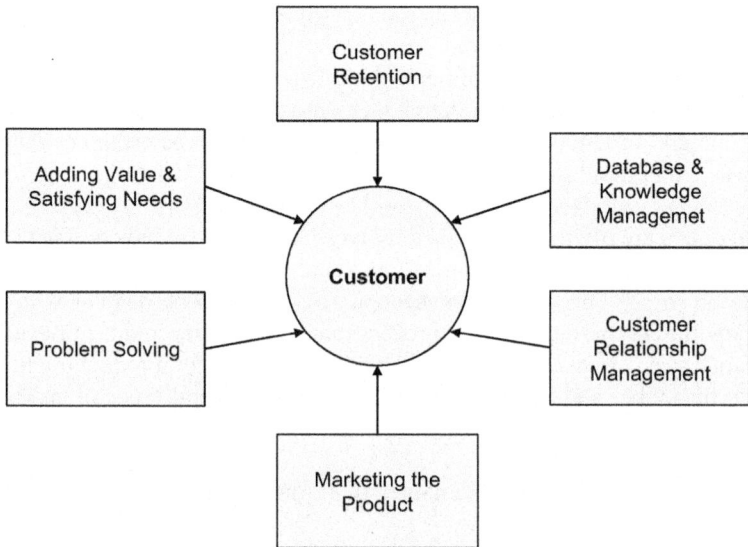

Fig. 2.2 Factors of modern selling [Source: Adapted from Moncrief and Marshall (2005, p. 19)]

management, analysis of market information, recruitment, and training). Successful selling is a multifaceted activity.

- *Problem solving*: The traditional view of the salesperson is to see the customer, to persuade to buy, and to walk away with the order. This "hit-and-run sale" belongs to the past. Nowadays, successful salespeople often act as a consultant. They work with the customer to identify problems, determine needs, and propose and implement effective solutions. This is what customers are looking for: An individualized solution that suits their needs.
- *Adding value and satisfying needs*: From the above it follows that modern salespeople must have the ability to identify and later to satisfy the customers' needs. It is often the case that customers do not recognize that they have a need (the so-called latent need). Therefore, it is the salesperson's job to stimulate need recognition and to make customers aware of the improvements being created and made available by implementing the solution at hand (i.e., higher productivity, reduced costs, remain innovative). In doing so, the salesperson will have added value to the customer's business, and the buyer in person.
- *Customer retention*: According to the old 80:20 rule, 80% of the business is coming from 20% of the customers. This means that salespeople should devote considerable resources to retain existing highly profitable customers. Key account management (KAM) has therefore become an important form of sales organization. It means that a salesperson or team focuses on one or a few major customers only. It is for this reason that numerous companies apply the ABC (customer) analysis which divides the customers of a company into A, B, and C customers according to their relevance. The application is explained in Sect. 6.1.3. However, companies should not forget prospecting and winning new customers. While you read these lines, a competitor of yours is trying to get your customers on board!
- *Database and knowledge management*: Today, much of the sales and marketing strategy revolves around the development, maintenance, and use of a customer database. It allows the company to better serve its customer base. Despite the experience in the field, salespeople should for sure be expected to contribute knowledge to the database. In addition, they should collect as much data as possible, given the current possibilities to use and process "big data." In return, they also gain broad customer knowledge.

2.2   The Sales Arena

Sales managers and salespeople are operating in a very complex environment marked by technological changes, shifting customer demands, and strong competition. It is becoming ever more difficult for companies to handle their sales activities. We believe it is necessary to create a *quintessential Sales Arena* in which the sales process, the most relevant instruments and tools, and the way these elements interact are described. With this map, it will be possible for any sales manager to fulfill his

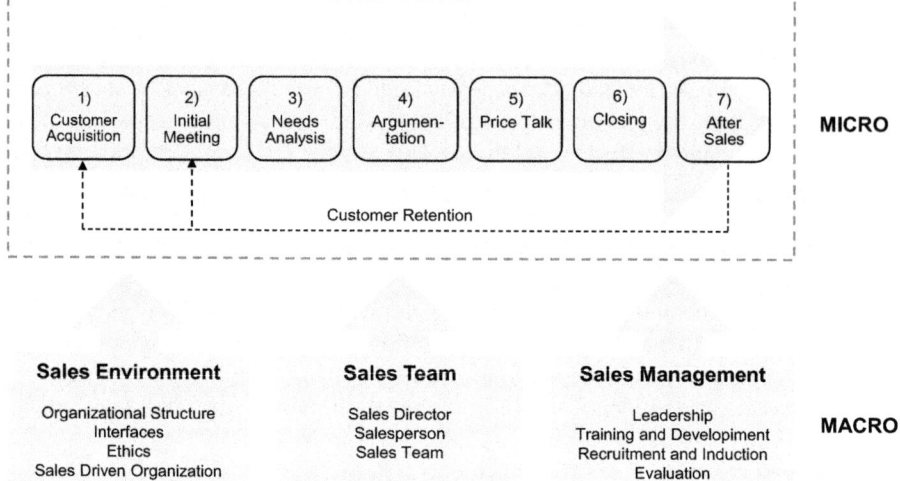

Fig. 2.3 Sales Arena

tasks more efficiently than before. Figure 2.3 presents the ideal sales process of a company. Each salesperson follows a repeated set of actions with a given prospect to move him from an early-stage prospect to a joint customer. This in the individual level or as we call it: *micro-level*. Sales managers and sales reps must have the skills related to each stage in order to close more deals and increase revenue. Random acts will only produce random and uncertain results. Only a systematic and well-defined personal selling approach can assure predictable results.

Furthermore, Fig. 2.3 presents three factors on *macro-level* that interact with the sales process—the sales environment, the sales team, and the sales management. Both are crucial to the ultimate success of a company, because they shape and determine nearly all interactions with the firm's customers. As organization and leadership are essential functions of sales directors and managers, they will be the structural guidance of the main chapters.

References

Jobber, D., & Lancaster, G. (2012). *Selling and sales management* (9th ed.). Harlow: Pearson Education.

Kreutzer, R., Rumler, A., & Wille-Baumkauff, B. (2014). *B2B-Online-Marketing und Social Media. Ein Praxisleitfaden*. Wiesbaden: Springer Gabler.

Moncrief, W. C., & Marshall, G. W. (2005). The evolution of the seven steps of selling. *Industrial Marketing Management, 34*(1), 13–22.

Ziglar, Z. (2003). *Ziglar on selling. The ultimate handbook for the complete sales profession*. Nashville, TN: Thomas Nelson.

The Sales Process

3

Sales is often seen as a very individual, flexible profession. And a lot of sales reps in a lot of companies take it as their quality standard, to approach their customers and prospects in a unique individual way. So far, so good.

The—in fact—inefficient point is that the majority of those "flexible" salespeople use this de facto favorable goal (i.e., to be close to the customer) just to cover that they are freestylers. They do believe that a clear structure would cut off their performance and limit it to an average performance level. So their aim is mainly not to make a 100% tailor-made approach but more to live their own business style and not to adapt to certain guidelines. And as we know from economics of scale, producing unique products is in view of margins often not the most efficient way.

Our experience—and this has been proved in the Far East and "Wild" West—is different. We strongly support the way that structure is not a contradiction but a synergetic aspect of a professional sales approach. It helps the company to organize itself more efficiently: e.g., to set forecasts, to gather the most effective arguments and door openers, and to track all activities. For the individual, structure reduces complexity, it clarifies the follow-up activities, and it develops a significant higher skill level. By the way: Professional sports (like soccer, tennis, or basketball) could not achieve a high level of performance without having a precise match plan in place. So the task is to be flexible (as a company and as a sales rep) and to be empathic within a certain structure.

The main idea of the sales process that is shown in the following is: The more personal—the more efficient. Of course, this personal approach may be sometimes impossible due to the size of the sales reps' sales territory or the limited travel budget. Salespeople should always choose *the most personal approach possible*. In terms of priority, this means: personal meeting, then Skype conference, and then call. Emails which are pretty strong used today—especially in technical companies—are easy to produce as well as easy to delete and do not have much impact as stand-alone tool.

The first great issue is the sales process. Although there are diverse types of customers, prospects, products, services, and sales situations, there are only seven

© Springer International Publishing AG 2018
S. Hase, C. Busch, *The Quintessence of Sales*, Quintessence Series,
DOI 10.1007/978-3-319-61174-7_3

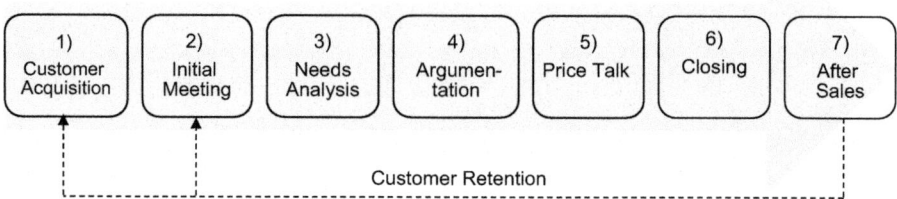

Fig. 3.1 The sales process

basic but interacting steps that form the personal sales process. The process is outlined in Fig. 3.1.

Once the appointment with a new prospect has been scheduled, the salesperson continues from one step to the next step. Stage 7, however, is not the end of the sales process but rather the new beginning. The back office's or the salesperson's follow-up and service activities should generate repeat sales or purchase of new products or services. The rule of thumb in sales is that it costs three to five times as much to acquire a new customer as to keep an existing customer from leaving (Turner & Shah, 2010). Hence, it would be smart to focus time and money in keeping the existing customers satisfied. The sales process begins anew.

In the following section, we discuss the seven steps of the sales process in more detail. In this respect, we also introduce the most important selling techniques that salespeople need to know and to apply to be successful in sales.

3.1   Customer Acquisition

Prospecting and Qualifying
Customers are continually leaving the company for many reasons including bankruptcy, relocation, or switching to other suppliers. It is common for a company to lose 15–20% of customers each year (Tschohl, 2008). To increase or at least maintain sales volume, salespeople must continually search for *new prospects*. The first step in the sales process is therefore to obtain leads. A *qualified lead* is basically the complete name (including pre- and surname), postal and personal email address (not "info@..."), or telephone number of a person which potentially requires the seller's products or services. Before putting time and energy into a prospect, it is recommended to further qualify the lead. In line with Hair, Anderson, Mehta, and Babin (2010), we suggest that salespeople—or in bigger enterprises the so-called "sales back office"—qualify it in terms of Authority to buy? Money to buy? Eligibility to buy? When people and companies have passed all screens, they become prospects for a sales call.

Acquiring New Customers

In general, there are plenty of ways to get in contact with a prospect. Trade fairs, exhibitions, speaker's opportunities, print, radio or TV ads, Internet presence, etc., are useful tools to get in touch with potential customers. In recent years, direct mails have been quite popular, which have been partly replaced by newsletters and digital mass emails in the last years.

What we do focus on in the following are acquisition techniques that the sales representative (in the following sales rep) can personally influence. This is mainly: *Cold calls* and—although decreasingly—cold visits. As the Internet has significantly changed the business setup, cold visits are today more seen as a sign of non-efficient time management. For that reason, we will focus on cold calling.

Acquiring customers by cold calling is one of the most difficult tasks for salespeople. *Typical performance issues* include first of all the *inner attitude*. Many salespeople—that, by the way, is also true for successful key account managers—have negative feelings toward calling prospects. The reasons for that are manifold. Hearing a "No" pretty frequently; feeling constant pressure to set appointments and make revenue; and being negatively influenced by family, friends, or society are the main reasons. The consequence is that salespeople start to conjure up "excuses" why they do not make cold calls today but better tomorrow, or they may persuade themselves that the prospect will say "NO!" either way. Just to name a few. If this is the case, salespeople need to work on their attitude. It is always a question of decision—we decide: Am I really committed to what I do? The positive attitude (to be discussed in Sect. 5.2.2) makes half the battle of the sales call.

A second typical performance issue is *making the "right offer"* to the prospect. If a salesperson starts like "We are ... We have ... We can ...," he is probably the wrong partner for us because we always ask ourselves "What's in for us?." For that reason, sales reps preferably put together the "door opener" from the decision maker's perspective before they make the call. The goal is to arouse interest for meeting in person to discuss the matter individually.

Handling objections is a third typical performance issue. In most cases, the decision makers will first have an objection to the appointment request in order to "test" the salesperson (Is it really worth it?) or because he is simply busy. At this point of the call, many salespeople fail because they do not convince with commitment and added value or they give up after the second round of objection. The best is to view it as a "quality check." To overcome the objection, it is recommended that sales reps (1) show understanding for the underlying situation, (2) show the decision maker his personal added value, and (3) to repeat the date proposed in a confident manner. If he still refuses to meet after 2–3 objection rounds, it is best to finish the call and follow-up several weeks/months later. The classical structure of a cold call is shown in Table 3.1.

Performance Tips for Customer Acquisition

Here are a few points that salespeople should consider when making cold calls:

- Argue always and consistently from the customer's perspective: "you" instead of "we."

Table 3.1 Structure of customer acquisition (Cold call)

0. Positive attitude: I *really like* to call somebody new (not: I *must*)	5. Handling objections: "No time," "We are satisfied," "No need"...
1. Preparation: Using guidelines and warming up before the call	6a. If YES: Scheduling appointment
2. Professional greeting	6b. IF NO: Follow-up in x weeks
3. Making an convincing "offer": Let's meet, because...!	7. Saying goodbye
4. Suggesting a precise time and date: on ... at ... am/pm	8. Documentation in CRM system

- Prepare good "door openers," also called "hooks," and know your facts and figures. Do not be generic: "We have great know-how. ..." Instead, be distinctive: "Due to our know-how from 10 years, over 100 projects and 20 industries, you'll find your way to boost your sales by at least 8% within 1 year."
- Arouse interest! No technical discussion on the phone. Everything will be discussed in detail during the meeting.
- Communicate on eye level: Not too submissive. No "would" or "could". No "maybe".
- Make a precise and binding offer: "I like to meet you next Tuesday at 10 am."
- Show value!
- Repeat the date and time proposed: "I therefore like to meet you: Tuesday, at 10 am." This shows your confidence!
- Enjoy it genuinely and start today.

3.2   Initial Meeting

The first personal contact is of huge importance. Today, some call "the opening" even "the new closing." It can create (besides the technical level) a chemistry that is designed to shape something for a loyal, long-lasting business relation: *Trust!* So it is quite surprising that many salespeople do not take the immediate opportunity to meet their counterpart as early as possible. They often prefer writing emails and doing phone calls instead. In our everyday life, we have attended hundreds of closing meetings where both parties just met for the very first time. That's unprofessional and the results often speak for themselves.

In fact, salespeople make their critical—often long-lasting— impressions during the first face-to-face contact with the prospect. So it is important to consider the ways in which a favorable response can be achieved. First of all, buyers expect sales reps to be businesslike in their personal appearance and behavior. Simple things like an underdressed or sloppy outfit, untidy hair, and bad breath are likely to create a bad impression. This should be a classical no-brainer, but it's still astonishing how often this happens in the field.

Customer appointments therefore begin when salespeople come into the "field of view" (parking area) of the customer. Some customers welcome a potential business partner by spotting him out of the window to get an "unvarnished" impression of that person. Therefore, it is recommended to have all documents ready at hand and to dispense with cigarettes, chewing gum, and so on.

The opening has become even more important than it ever was since it sets the tone for the rest of the sales process. As the idiom says, "pressure creates counterpressure." The same counts for building sympathy: "A smile creates another smile." If the salesperson connects with the conversational partner on an emotional level, it is much easier for the buyer to answer the seller's questions. Why? Sympathy for each other leads to a relaxed and open meeting atmosphere, which in turn leads to better and more concrete needs analysis, which in turn leads to a "tailor-made" offer, which in turn increases the likelihood of winning the contract. As a conclusion, the *emotional level* is the basis for prospering customer relationships.

To achieve sympathy and build trust, salespeople should have a credible and authentic appearance and should open with a smile, a firm handshake, and *small talk*. The latter aspect is not to be underestimated. If we do not know the salesperson yet, we always ask ourselves—wittingly or unwittingly—"Can I trust him?" The buyer will not find an answer to this question by looking at the salesperson's technical expertise, but by looking at the personal level instead. Salespeople should therefore use a professional warm-up to mitigate rejection, to affirm the relationship, and to soften the parting. Some small talk topics that are considered to be "safe" in most circumstances include travel, weather, sports, hobbies, and—not to forget—the customer's office. For example, if salespeople have to wait for a short while at the client's reception, they could pay attention to interior design, awards, trophies, product samples, customer magazines, and so on. These are good points that salespeople can refer back to in small talk situations. Important: The prospect or customer must notice that the salesperson has a genuine interest in the customer, his subjects, and the meeting.

A *sovereign "bridge" from small talk to needs analysis* (the next step of the selling process) is important so that the emotional level and therefore the positive energy level is not lost. Far too many salespeople come to an abrupt end and start with the technical discussion (e.g., "Well, let's talk about. . ."). In these cases, the appreciation of customers is rapidly lost (i.e., "I knew it—he only wants me to buy something"). Professional salespeople build an elegant bridge by taking up a point of the small talk topic and "bridging" to the topic of the meeting. After professionally clarifying the time and agenda of the meeting, the salesperson can start with the needs assessment. The classical structure of a first meeting is shown in Table 3.2.

Performance Tips for Initial Meetings

Here are a few points that salespeople should consider when having a first customer meeting:

Table 3.2 Structure of initial meeting

0. Preparation	• Search for information • Define goal and match plan • Have a positive attitude!
1. Professional greeting	• Have a winning appearance • Adjust approach and dress code to target group • Open with a smile and handshake
2. Invitation for small talk	• Offer a topic—proactively • Make him speak • Have genuine interest
3. Sovereign bridge	• Switch elegantly to business • Look for clue words

4. "Setting the scene"	• Propose the agenda of the current meeting
	  – Customer talks first about his company and needs ($\rightarrow$ step 5)
	  – Then you present possible solutions ($\rightarrow$ step 6)
	  – Next steps ($\rightarrow$ 7)
	• Ask whether customer is ok with that running order

5. Professional talk	• Conduct a needs analysis
6. Possible solution to problem	• Discuss possible solutions • Use wording of a benefit argumentation
7. Follow-up (next steps)	• Agree on action plan: Who does what until when?
8. Outro	• Upgrade: Use the same small talk topic ("smart talk") • Say goodbye

- Be punctual.
- Be prepared: What do you know about the contact person and his company? What can you offer? What are possible objections? What is your goal? What is your inner attitude?
- Be proactive and start the small talk. The product or service comes with the salesperson. Sympathy and trust is therefore key.
- Offer (as a host) or accept (as a guest) a coffee or another beverage to establish a relaxed, open meeting atmosphere.
- Set the scene: Propose an agenda and double check the time frame. This helps you to structure the meeting.
- Do not forget to agree on an action plan. No meeting without precise follow-up!
- Upgrade: Do "smart talk" before you say goodbye. What we mean by that is: Use the same small talk topic. If you talked about rock music right in the beginning, then talk about it again before you leave. This shows genuine interest in the other person and any information that is being provided.

3.3   Needs Analysis

In every customer communication and, of course, in all meetings, salespeople are dependent on the obtained information of their conversational partners. The more they know, the more likely they will be able to meet the specific concerns and "pain points" of the customer. Only in this way, they can create a *customized offer*. Also, they can underline their own competence—more or less convincingly—by asking high-quality questions. Salespeople should show their conversational partners that they are committed toward a "tailor-made" cooperation. The more convinced the customer is by this conversation, the less is the price the center of the argument later on.

The needs analysis is of central importance and a classical bottleneck for almost every company. Because this part requires both professional listening and speaking abilities as well as a lot of empathy. That includes a very sophisticated listening mode (to hear "buzz words" between the lines, like: "We are *quite* satisfied so far"), quick dialogue abilities and precise wording, as well as consistent and ongoing questions. From our experience in the field around the globe, the needs assessment is one of the crucial differentiators when it comes to professional selling. For this particular reason, you will find some wording examples in the following paragraphs to stress the importance.

Another important remark which has to be made at this stage: Many companies—particularly big players—have at this point a strong addiction of doing upfront presentations before conducting a needs assessment. They like to immediately present their products or services. This results in a straight demo mode—without knowing the real needs of the prospect. Shifting this upfront-presenting mode into a much more up-to-date and effective *listening mode* is often part of a professional sales approach.

Note: Slide presentations may be useful and should be conducted—if required—after the needs analysis. It is part of the benefit argumentation as discussed in the following chapter.

Urgent Needs and Pain Points
What is required to reduce the lead time significantly, so that a customer or prospect buys now? What do you think? When we ask these questions, most sales reps say: "The customer has to have a need." Well, yes, but that is today in the time of postponing investments not enough. It has to be nowadays an *urgent need*. This means that the customer notices and acknowledges the pain he has and understands that an immediate action is required to solve the problem or question at hand.

There are two ways in which this urgent need is being identified. Usually the *sales rep* sees the urgent need—because he is the expert! Nearly 80% of salespeople, based on our experience, see the customer's problem and suggest a possible solution right away ("You need solution A!!"). However, from a selling point of view, this method is not promising. Many offers fail at this point.

Like we mentioned in Chap. 2, prospects become more cautious due to increasing competition, transparency, and bad experience. The problem is that salespeople are often too fast. They already speak about problems and possible solutions—which is an investment for the prospect—when the counterpart has not even realized where his problem lies.

Think about yourself: If you would meet an IT consultant for the first time, and after 3 min of conversation, he tells you straight away that you have to invest into

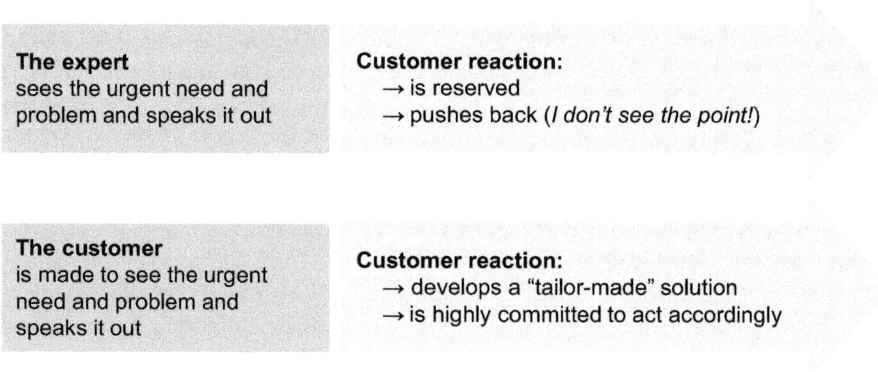

| The expert
sees the urgent need and
problem and speaks it out | Customer reaction:
→ is reserved
→ pushes back (*I don't see the point!*) |

| The customer
is made to see the urgent
need and problem and
speaks it out | Customer reaction:
→ develops a "tailor-made" solution
→ is highly committed to act accordingly |

Fig. 3.2 Seeing the urgent need

completely new hard- and software. What would be your reaction? We guess that you would "normally" not be amused, think it over, and postpone your decision.

So, not the salesperson should call attention to the urgent need but the customer! He himself must see an urgent need in the conversation. To proceed with our example: When I realize by myself: "Indeed our software is out-dated, we can't run certain standards due to limited data capacity, the hardware is much too old and we can't perform central topics of our business model, which costs us x Euro a week," then I do understand the need for updating the entire IT.

What we want to say with this example: The customer was not persuaded into buying (i.e., doing the update). Instead, he (1) realized by himself that he has a problem; (2) identified the consequences if nothing changes; and finally (3) comes up with a solution that he wants to implement, and fast—as the customer has seen the urgent need. Figure 3.2 illustrates the two ways of identifying the urgent need:

What does it mean for salespeople? They have to transform their expertise into *questions*. For a lot of technically affine people (e.g., engineers), this is a big mind shift because they originally regard questions as being weak and rate immediate answers given as a high level of competence.

Instead of seeing the urgent need and speaking it out by themselves, the salesperson *asks* the customer questions that identify the problem and the impact—and later on even a professional solution. In this way, the prospect or customer sees the pain point and is highly committed with regard to the solution. As experience teaches, only 20% of salespeople ask questions and do good needs analysis before coming up with possible solutions.

Ten Points for Conducting a Needs Assessment

From our experience, the needs assessment will take depending on the complexity of the product or service about 20–120 min. It is important that salespeople note the following:

1. Connect with the customer on an emotional level (i.e., small talk) before you start with asking questions.
2. Clarify the time frame: Is still the agreed time available? It would be a shame if the prospect cancels the meeting in the middle for follow-up appointments. Adapt if time is shortened.
3. Tell the other party that you have prepared some questions for the interview and to ask him for permission to ask these to demonstrate him that you are interested in a productive cooperation.
4. Begin slowly: Prospective customers are not accustomed to be asked and need to gain confidence.
5. Start with questions about general status quo (company, products, etc.) and work your way gradually to specific information (requirements, problems, consequences, etc.). If the conversational partner does not know you, he will not tell you of any problems and goals right away. An overview is given in Fig. 3.3.
6. Listen carefully to buzzwords (e.g., "slightly," "little," "apparently"). Hardly anybody will immediately agree to have problems—they make it sound much softer.
7. Actively lead the conversation. If you do not, the buyer takes over.
8. Make sure that you keep up the dialogue! The best questions will not help, if the conversation feels like a bit of an interrogation.
9. Take notes. The answers of prospective customers are the evidence of your offer and may be extremely important for the next steps in the sales process.
10. Do not "go too fast" in the problem-solving mode! First, it is important to work out the pain points of the conversational partner.

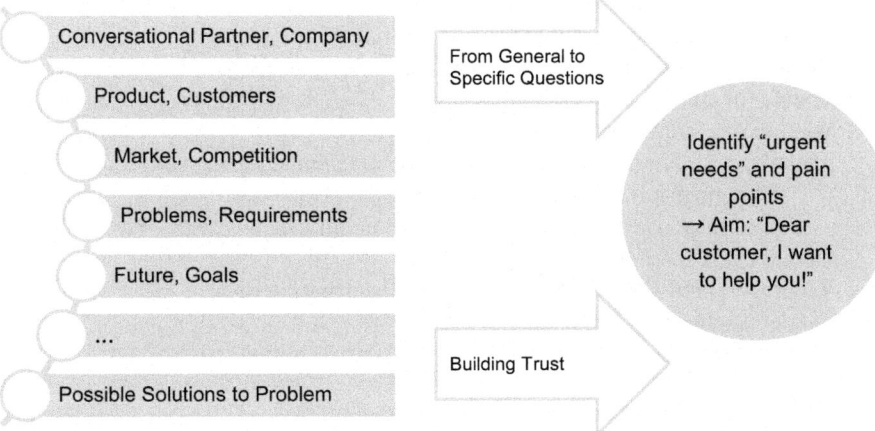

Fig. 3.3 Possible categories to conduct a needs analysis

Questioning Techniques
The use of questions and the possibilities of variation decide highly on the success or failure of the conversation. Questioning techniques are the key to the required information of your conversational partner. A skillful questioning technique will bring salespeople many advantages. It sounds easy but it's like facing a delicious lobster and you do not simply know how to open it. In fact, there are some good approaches that one can follow (e.g., SPIN® selling, which was first developed by Neil Rackham (1988) and Huthwaite International). In sum: It's in practical terms more a question of routine and listening skills rather than of intellectual capacity. The questioning technique:

- Gives the conversational partner the feeling that you listen with interest to him
- Makes it easy to change the direction of the conversation
- Helps identify buying motives in the conversation
- Enables to recognize counter arguments faster
- Allows a "diplomatic" correction of arguments of the prospect or customer
- Creates the necessary basis of trust with the prospect or customer
- Helps to better judge the prospect or customer
- Makes it easier to parry unfair attacks
- Gives time to formulate the next thought

Basic Questioning Techniques In practice, a wide variety of questions may be used during a needs assessment such as sharp angle questions, opinion gathering questions, and inclusion questions (see DeCormier and Jobber (1993) for details). If salespeople still have trouble with identifying specific customer needs, we suggest that they first use open and closed questions only:

- *Open questions* are the heart of a customer-oriented questioning technique. The conversational partner has maximum freedom in answering. The challenge of the salesperson is not to lose the thread, because he does not know how the prospect will answer him. Open questions ("Who? What? Where? When? Why? How?", etc.) are helpful:
  - To collect and organize information—central in the needs assessment
  - To define problems and develop solutions
- *Closed questions*: The conversation partner can only answer with "Yes" or "No." Closed questions are good:
  - To be sure that we have understood the information right
  - To define intermediate results
  - To come to a decision and to "close" the entire conversation

It may sound easy, but in daily business even many very experienced salespeople have trouble to assess the prospects' real pain points. First of all, it is important to really control the entire conversation phase with good questions. This requires practice and the withdrawal of the natural urge to offer a solution right away.

Advanced Questioning Techniques   Making a good need-gap analysis is the art of posing excellent questions at the right time. The aim is that the customer (Not the salesperson!) asks: "That's interesting and how can we solve it?." To get him to this point, the salesperson must work out concrete facts and figures to let him "feel" the urgent need. Four advanced questioning techniques can be used:

- *Starter questions*: As discussed, salespeople should always start with short (sic!) open questions to activate the customer and to enhance the chance to get the "big points." They can ask customers about knowledge, opinions, and/or feelings. Asking the "why?" question is great—if you ask this question five times, you definitely understand the true reason or cause of the problem. However, salespeople should be careful with using this wording because dialogue partners may feel criticized or driven in the corner. We therefore suggest to change the wording, for instance: "What is the reason for. . ."?.
- *Status quo questions*: This kind of questions helps to understand the entire situation of the counterpart. Often, prospects and customers do not know yet that they currently have an urgent need (the so-called latent need). We actively need to show them that they have a big problem that needs to be solved. In this case, we recommend that sales reps ask their customers all about the current situation in order to drill deeper and to derive the problem.
- *"Log-in" questions*: We call these questions "log-in" questions, because salespeople show that they listen and want to understand the customer's situation exactly. These questions are also useful when dialogue partners do not go into detail. For instance, they say: "We need to do more" or "The customer service could be better." We recommend that salespeople dive deeper to find out exact facts and figures. By asking: "When you say 'We need to do more,' what do you mean concretely by that?," you will be very surprised what customers start talking about.
- *Impact questions*: Through these questions, the effects and consequences will be felt by the customer. What will happen if the customer's problem is not solved? Typical examples of impact questions are: "How does the delivery bottleneck affect you currently?" or "What additional costs resulted by the high consumption?." By asking these questions, the customer notices the pain he has and understands that an action is required to solve the problem or question at hand.

Conclusion: Only the one who asks the right question gets a good answer and identifies *real* pain points! For that reason, we have summarized the questioning techniques in Table 3.3.

Developing a High-Qualified Questionnaire

Salespeople can create a tailor-made offer on the basis of high-quality questions that identify the concerns and pain points of the customer. To achieve this, we recommend that salespeople develop a catalogue of questions, which covers all categories that are necessary to make a customized offer. For instance: conversational partner, company, customers, and future. The below list of questions will

Table 3.3 Questioning techniques to identify pain points

1. *Starter questions* • What. . . • How. . . • When. . . • Where. . .	*or* From general topics. . .
2. *Status quo questions* (current situation) • What do you believe is the reason for "x"? • What is in your view the cause for "y"? • When did "x" start? • How often does "x" occur?	
3. *"Log-in" questions* • When you say "x," what do you mean concretely by that? • For my understanding, what does "y" mean in numbers? (e.g., x EUR costs, x days late delivery)	
4. *Impact questions* (current and future consequences) • How does "x" affect you currently? • What is the consequence if you continue this way? • What are the estimated costs of "x"? • What is the impact of "y"?	. . . to specific pain points!

give you some suggestions and ideas to start developing your own list of questions for the needs assessment (see Table 3.4). If you like, ask yourself:

1. Which of these questions, can you use for your own questionnaire?
2. What additional questions and/or categories are still missing?

Performance Tips for Needs Assessment

Here are a few points that sales reps should consider when conducting a needs analysis:

- Maintain a good emotional level. Otherwise, you will find yourself in an "interrogation." And this will destroy the relationship with your prospective client or customer.
- Ask high-qualified questions, listen actively, and make notes.
- Dive deeper to actually derive "pain points" by using "log-in" questions, status quo questions, and impact questions.
- Ask for facts and figures to derive pain points: "High costs" versus "100,000 EUR costs" or "Late delivery" versus "3 weeks late delivery." You see the difference?
- Do not "go too fast" in the problem-solving mode.

Table 3.4 Developing a high-qualified questionnaire

Conversational partner	*Company*
• How long are you actually working for this company	• From your point of view, what are your company's distinctive values?
• For how long are you already familiar with the topic "x"/in this company?	• What makes your company special?
• To begin with, could you please introduce yourself in two or three sentences?	• How is your turnover allocated to your branches "x," "y," "z"?
Customer's customer	*Future, goals*
• What is your current customer structure like?	• Compared to today. What will be different in the end of 20xx in terms of...?
• Could you please briefly describe: What are your customer's needs and requirements, if he would like to make business with you?	• What do you like to achieve within the next 6, 12, 24, 36 months?
• When you talk to your customers: What do they say why they like working with you?	• What milestones are necessary to reach your goals? How far are you actually within this process?

3.4 Argumentation

After asking the prospect or customer goal-oriented questions to uncover needs and pain points, the salesperson can now present precisely products and services that will best satisfy those specific needs. There are in general three different levels of argumentation:

- Feature
- Advantage
- Benefit

Features are clear product or service characteristics (i.e., spec sheet). An example is "This car is equipped with an anti-lock braking system." The sales effect of features on an interested party is relatively neutral. Nevertheless, it is astonishing how many sales reps do not even use these kind of hard facts.

Advantages demonstrate how a product characteristic—a feature, in other words—can be employed effectively to help the user. Most advantages can be expressed in the following manner:

- "Due to ... (the feature x), you can ..."
- "Thanks to ... (the feature x), you can ..."
- "With ... (the feature x), you can ..."

An advantage is, for example: "Thanks to the anti-lock braking system, you can even keep control of your vehicle on wet road surfaces, as the system prevents the wheels from locking, even if you need to brake sharply." Hence, advantages are clearly more convincing than features in a sales context.

Benefits illustrate in which way a product feature corresponds to the individual need of the purchaser. This level of argumentation is even more convincing than the advantage level. The reason is that an interested party purchases, in principle, because he has a definite need. The probability of a contract being concluded is at its greatest if the sales rep directs his argumentation toward this specific need. As a result, the benefit argumentation is the most effect way of describing a product or service. In addition, it is the only way to differentiate successfully in B2B markets. We will therefore focus on benefits in the following section.

Presenting Benefits

After conducting the needs assessment, the sales rep can now present precisely the benefits out of the particular product or service. This is the immediate second step (a "twin") and should follow straight after conducting the needs analysis. The prospect now knows that he has to solve his problem (which he sometimes did not even know before the meeting). He is open and also will ask the sales rep about his recommendation. Note: This could also be the time to present a tailor-made slide show.

Now, it is "delivery time" for the salesperson. He stimulates the desire for the offering by highlighting the benefits being offered to the prospect or the customer. Product features and advantages are important only if they can be tied directly to a specific benefit the prospect is seeking. For example, pointing out a battery service life of 12 h (i.e., feature) when demonstrating a cell phone does not mean much to a prospect unless he said during needs analysis that he is traveling a lot and using the device excessively. The salesperson should therefore make sure to know his products and services inside out and to describe only the ones that are relevant to the prospect or customer.

Customer Values and Benefits

To give a better understanding, how many features does a car have? Correct, x thousand. But only a few are really important to us when buying a car. And every buyer brings up other car features that are essential to him. Just these few compelling points (typically 2–4) need to be identified in the needs assessment. The benefit argumentation helps salespeople to argue these points with a maximum conviction. A benefit is always individual and leaves the purely technical level of the product. The customer thus gets 100% custom solution based on his own needs. Its aim is to provide the prospect and customer with the feeling that he found in us—the seller— exactly the right solution and was understood.

When sales reps use this level of argumentation, a prospect or customer cannot make an objection because *he told* the sales rep during the needs analysis that *he has a specific problem* that needs to be solved. The sales rep has the solution for that. For that reason, the prospect or customer can only make an objection about the price—but not about the tailor-made solution. Fig. 3.4 sums up the characteristics of a benefit:

Fig. 3.4 Characteristics of a benefit

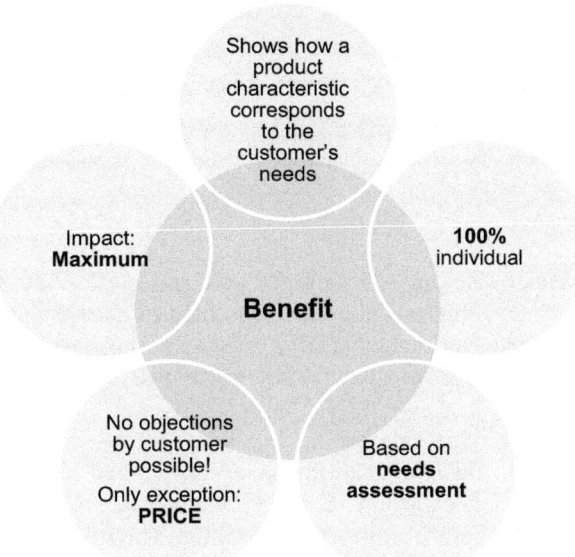

Shows how a product characteristic corresponds to the customer's needs

Impact: **Maximum**

100% individual

Benefit

No objections by customer possible!
Only exception: **PRICE**

Based on **needs assessment**

Benefit Argumentation

When the salesperson has completed the needs assessment, he can offer the solution available in clear benefit statements. The general structure of the benefit argumentation is shown in Table 3.5.

Performance Tips for Benefit Argumentation

The structure of the benefit argumentation sounds easy, but in practice it is not. Each single word can make a difference in convincing—or not convincing—the customer. This requires good speaking abilities, practice, and self-reflection. Here are a few points that salespeople should consider:

- Argue always from the customer's perspective: "You" instead of "We."
- Pay attention to a convincing body language. These few points can decide in case of doubt about the order.
- Do not pack all "pain points" in the first argument. You will have shot your bolt, before negotiation has even started.
- Talk to prospective and customers directly. Avoid statements like "The customer saves. . .."
- Get the prospect agree that your offering will remove his pains.

3.5 Price Talk

When it comes to price talk, the heart beats faster on the sales side. In every sales circle, there will be (hopefully) this moment of truth. Many professional buyers ask for the "price tag" much earlier in the process. The sales task is—as we have

Table 3.5 Structure of a benefit argumentation

1. Refer back and start with a specific customer statement from the needs analysis	3. Bring in your solution by telling the customer how a specific product feature meets his need
2. Repeat the problem and remind him of the resulting effects (as the idiom says, "to bring up a painful subject")	4. Make a convincing conclusion by demonstrating the positive consequences

discussed before—to stand the heat and speak about the customer's urgent needs and pain points and about the presented solution and its benefits first. Only then, the sales rep can demonstrate a persuasive price–performance ratio. Prices are the logical result of the salesperson's performance—in both ways—positive or negative.

The buying side has made a lot of efforts in last years to shift the balance of power in their favor in this central topic and to gain leadership in order to earn margin (i.e., call for tenders, anonym bidding, frequent change of buyers). What we focus on here is still a B2B meeting. The interesting thing is: Price is mainly a matter of individual perception and identification. Therefore, we like to give you five short but effective main ideas about the function of price.

Fundamental Ideas About the Price

Price talks are an integral part of the sales conversation. As many salespeople think of price and price objections as a bad thing or the result of a bad performance before, we first of all like to share some fundamental ideas about the "price":

1. *Price objections are today part of "the game"*: In Chap. 2, we discussed the increasing role of the purchase order department and their reason for being: It is nowadays in a lot of companies as stated in their internal code of conduct a "must" to ask 3–4 suppliers and to go for lower prices. Those companies who do not ask for discounts—and let it be rhetorical—are often not really interested. Salespeople should therefore have a positive attitude toward price objections!
2. *The price is mainly determined by the sales professional himself and his inner attitude*: A price issue–like "my product is too expensive"—will be unconsciously carried over to the discussion partner. If the salesperson does not stand behind the price, how should his prospect develop an appreciation for it? As a result: Salespeople need to identify with their price—or adapt it to their (argumentation) level.
3. *Price is never objective but always subjective*: What seems to be expensive for one company/person may be perceived as cheap for another person. Since products are not comparable with one another in terms of its subjective perception (color, shape, operating comfort, etc., are perceived differently), there is no objective expensive or cheap!
4. *Price fulfils a function*: Prospects deduce—sometimes unconsciously—higher product quality from higher prices. True to the motto: "What costs nothing is

worth nothing" and "Quality has its price." Therefore, the product value is always closely related to the price.

5. *High prices are rarely a reason for denying*: Practice shows that the prices of market leaders are normally significantly higher than the average prices in the industry. Products with low prices are often in fact—despite good quality—difficult to sell.

Seven Points for Stating and Negotiating the Price

The following guidelines will help salespeople to state and negotiate the price in a convincing manner. These aspects can decide in case of doubt about the order. If possible, prices should always be stated and negotiated in a personal meeting, and not via emails. The reason is that the salesperson—as a sales expert—is the strongest magnet to reason the price. So, let's go:

1. *Identify 100% with your price*. Otherwise, you transmit your anxiety about the price unconsciously to your conversational partner.
2. *Do not state the price too early*. Not even if the prospect or customer claims for it! Start with the "touch points" and explain the benefits before you state the price. Otherwise, there is a risk that the counterpart gets a "price shock," that is, he only thinks about the price, while you are talking about the value.
3. *State the price in a confident manner*—through the use of a clear and determined language and professional body language. Do not use conjunctives (i.e., would, could).
4. *Do not make a pause after stating the price*. Pauses have a boosting effect. As a result, the meaning of the price increases.
5. *Use the "sandwich method" instead*. It is best to repeat immediately before and after stating the price the benefits for your prospect or customer. Tell him again what he is all getting for his investment.
6. *Give a reason for the price*. The price is the sum of the prospect's or customer's benefits. This is part of handling price objections, which will be discussed hereinafter.
7. *Give discounts only with resistance*. Even if a discount is possible and taken into account. In case of giving a discount, ask your counterpart for a service in return.

Handling Price Objections

Even after an outstanding product and service presentation with well-articulated benefit argumentations, most prospects and customers are not ready to sign a purchase agreement. In fact, each of us understands that it is for private persons as well as buyers, managers, technical managers, etc., crucial to obtain the best possible value for money. Especially in the phase "price talk," however, the price is often decoupled from the actual product performance. The task of the salesperson is to prevent just that. Typical price objections are shown in Table 3.6.

First of all, the salesperson should listen and allow the prospect to describe his objection in full. Interrupting him is not only being rude but can also lead to loss of valuable information. When the salesperson is sure that he has understood

Table 3.6 Typical price objections

"The price is too high."	"The price isn't competitive."
"Competitor is x % cheaper."	"This price exceeds my budget by far."
"I cannot explain this to my supervisor."	"Lower it or you are out."
"I need a much better price."	"You earn so much on our account."
"You are higher than the competitor XYZ."	"You are too expensive."

Table 3.7 Structure for handling price objections

1. Showing understanding	3. Reconfirming the price
2. Diminishing the objection	

everything, he can go ahead and answer the objection. It is important to show the prospect that the offer described perfectly suits his needs and that the calculated price is absolutely worth the value. The structure of handling price objections is given below (Table 3.7).

Performance Tips for Price Talks

Here are a few points that salespeople should consider:

- Always state the exact price. Not: "The product costs approximately/about/circa . . .."
- Important: Do not give up too easy—sometimes other topics (such as security) hide behind the first price objections. Show at this point serious interest in a cooperation and that the customer is really important to you.
- Have in mind during price negotiation that the price is a normal part of "the game." Inner calmness decides.
- Work with the structure of handling price objections (see above) to return price objection.
- Insert the customer's specific compelling needs in your return answer.
- Confirm the price and show above all that the product is worth the price.
- Always take into account a small price reduction. Use the discount only, when it is absolutely necessary—and only after the third to fourth objection round. If you do it right in the beginning, the discussion partner will try to get out more.
- Always explain why you give a discount ("in order to win you as a new customer of our company"). If you do not, he will ask for the same price next time again.

Once the salesperson has answered the price objection, he should ensure that there are no further objections before moving on to next steps or closing the deal itself.

3.6   Closing

The more complex a product or service, the more sophisticated will be the sales process. From our experience, there is pretty often in selling capital goods a separate "closing round." This can occur also in addition to the price talk.

The selling techniques and skills discussed so far are not sufficient for consistent sales success. No matter how well the salesperson identifies the needs and pain points, explains the benefits of using the products and services, and overcomes price objections, there is likely to be some doubt present in the mind of the prospect or customer.

They may want to delay the decision, may want to think things over, or they just want to see what competitor x, y, and z has to offer. The problem of waiting another day is that it becomes more likely that the prospect or customer will buy from the competition. The salesperson should therefore use the situation, while he is there, and has this vital advantage over the competition. It is a central part of his job *to close the deal*. Such as in sports: The striker is always been measured by his goals.

So after reconfirming the own value for money during the price talk, it is now time to negotiate and to find a common conclusion. Beware of the following: Everybody, and especially the professional buyer wants to achieve a win in this game—otherwise they have failed from their company's point of view. The logic is: Let them win, too. This does not necessarily mean a monetary reduction. It can also be any personal or process-related details (i.e., the sales rep is the constant personal point of contact, shorter time of delivery, special requests, billing). Sales reps should take this into consideration for their own match plan.

Ten Key Elements of Closing the Deal
The following ten key elements of closing the deal may not be in the right order for the particular negotiation. However, they are absolutely relevant for significantly increasing the salesperson's closing rate.

1. *You are 100% positive about closing the deal*: Enter the final discussion with a positive attitude, calmness, confidence, and an appreciation for your offer. Think of your positive mindset: If you yourself do not believe in the contract, then who does?
2. *You act confident and determined*: Talk calmly and determined—avoid conjunctives (e.g., would, could), blowing smokes, and typical seller phrases. Think about your body language. Be the equivalent to your product: valuable, confident, competent, and reliable.
3. *You summarize the benefits for your prospect*: Repeat all points the other party has addressed by himself. Make matches. Get "yes" answers through tag questions. Caution: Do not use leading questions.
4. *You state the price in a steady and convincing manner*: The price is the logical consequence of your appearance and your argumentation. Therefore, it is important to have a certain language and body language in order to negotiate final obstacles. Price objections of prospective customers are nowadays the

norm. Be prepared and have "condition," i.e., argumentatively, for several price-rounds.

5. *You check for buying signals*: Pay attention—despite your own nervousness—to the prospect's verbal and nonverbal buying signals. Ask specific and targeted questions that will lead to partially or fully closing the deal.

6. *You diminish last doubts*: Help your prospect with conflicts in purchasing decisions. List his benefits together with him and eliminate step by step remaining concerns.

7. *You give your prospect a "cookie"*: Each customer likes to achieve a partial success ("small win")—whatever kind. Take this into account. And this does not always need to be a discount. Often, a qualitative accommodation to the needs of the customer (e.g., delivery time, special requests, configuration, and billing) is sufficient enough.

8. *You pose a closing question*: 90% of all sellers do not have the courage to ask directly about the job, because they are afraid to lose all chances in the event of rejection. This is an opportunity for the self-confident sales professional: "Can we close the deal now?"

9. *You get his signature today*: Do not put off the final decision until next week. What does the prospect prevent from signing now? A significant proportion of customers choose—despite their oral commitment—not to sign if they receive a longer period of time for making a final decision.

10. *You confirm the prospect's decision*: Do not give profuse thanks to your customer. Remove any possible buyer's remorse after he signed the contract. Confirm his decision, for example: "You have chosen really well" or "I congratulate you on this decision."

Performance Tips for Closing a Deal

Here are a few points that salespeople should consider:

* Understand the situation, motifs, and fears of the key decision makers.
* Be prepared—it is an integral part of any negotiation.
* Have a clear goal what you want to achieve at the end of negotiation.
* Ask directly for the order. A closed question implies a yes or no answer: "Would you like to buy it?."
* Make sure that you achieve a win–win situation.
* Do not sell something that they do not need. Ask yourself are you going for "one-shot" or long-lasting relationships?
* If prospects or customers say no—stay in contact. They may buy in a year or two.

3.7   After-Sales

Congratulations—you made the deal. Right after the decision maker has given his signature, the buyer's remorse sets in (De Gennaro, 2015). The bigger the deal—the bigger the question mark! So it is important that salespeople ensure that the "delivery" is on time. Everything happens exactly in the way it was promised before.

After making the sale, top salespeople do not disappear. Of course, the back office may take over to provide customer service such as installation and repair and to handle any customer complaints (see Table 3.8 for basic rules about customer complaints). However, successful sales reps stay in contact with the customer. It is far easier and less costly to keep present customers satisfied than to search out and acquire new customers (Hair et al., 2010).

On the one hand, it is much easier to work with and satisfy because the relationship has reached a level of trust and understanding about the customer's expectations. On the other hand, loyal customers will buy additional products and services and make recommendations to other prospects and potential clients. As a result, salespeople should frequently and properly follow up with customers to retain long-run, loyal, and profitable customers. The sales process begins anew.

As experiences teaches, if companies and salespeople perform under the best 10% of their branch, then there will be next orders. If they are simply average and have done—out of the customer's view—a lot of over-promise, then it might have been the last contract with this company. It is therefore recommended to double check the key performance indicators (KPIs) here (see Sect. 6.4 for qualitative and quantitative measures of performance) and to ask for references and communicate them.

Performance Tips for After Sales
Here are a few points that salespeople should consider:

- Make sure that you deliver what you promised.
- Go the extra mile: After you have made a sale, call your customer to check whether everything is OK. If it is, they will be pleased that you rang. If there is a problem, you can address it immediately and they will be delighted.

Table 3.8 Basic rules for handling customer complaints

1. Listen actively and patiently to customers' complaints—without interrupting
2. Do not argue with customers or take complaints personally
3. Empathize with the customers and try to see the situation from their point
4. Solve problems as fast as possible and fairly—even if the sale becomes unprofitable
5. Follow up to ensure that the complaint has been resolved to the customer's satisfaction
6. Keep records on complaints and their outcomes to spot patterns of problems

Source: Adapted from Hair et al. (2010)

- Stay in touch—via regular calls or personal meetings (Note: newsletters or mass emails do not count as after-sales)
- Be proactive. Do not wait until the customer calls you.
- Think about a good "hook" when you call your customers.
- Provide them for instance with interesting updates to their purchased products or services, precisely fitting topics, new trends, and/or studies.
- Listen and respond when customers have complaints.
- Respond to their phone calls and emails quickly.
- Arrange follow-up appointments to discuss subsequent orders. The sales process starts anew.

References

De Gennaro, A. (2015). Post-closing issues deserve attention to avoid optical buyer's remorse. *Ophthalmology Times, 40*(7), 69–70.

DeCormier, R. A., & Jobber, D. (1993). The counselor selling method. Concepts and constructs. *Journal of Personal Selling and Sales Management, 23*(4), 39–59.

Hair, J. F., Anderson, R. E., Mehta, R., & Babin, B. J. (2010). *Sales management. Building customer relationships and partnerships*. Mason, OH: South Western Cengage Learning.

Rackham, N. (1988). *SPIN selling*. New York: McGraw-Hill.

Tschohl, J. (2008). *Achieving excellence through customer service* (5th ed.). Minneapolis, MN: Best Sellers Publishing.

Turner, J., & Shah, R. (2010). *The top 10 things you must know about measuring ROI on social media marketing*. Upper Saddle River, NJ: Pearson Education.

The Sales Environment

4

After elaborating upon the micro perspective—i.e., how to manage the different personal skill requirements throughout an efficient sales process—we now change the point of view and enter the macro perspective. This means how the organization does deal with various influences coming from "outside." And how does it respond in terms of creating an efficient and adequate organizational framework to cope with these manifold requirements.

Having established good products and services as well as a structured sales process (see previous chapter) and a talented sales force (see subsequent chapter) is only half the battle. Because if it is missing the "right" organizational structure, interfaces, and flexibility, this will hardly lead in a bright and long-lasting economical future.

Analysts often use the so-called PESTLE analysis in order to describe a framework of macro-environmental factors. Broken down, it stands for political, economic, sociocultural, technological, legal, and environmental factors (Jobber & Lancaster, 2012). Some examples are given below:

- *Political*: globalization, stability, climate, type of government
- *Economic*: stability, growth of developing countries, foreign exchange rates
- *Sociocultural*: consumer behavior, educational background, career attitudes, cultural differences
- *Technological*: rate of change, telecommunications system, energy supply, transport infrastructure
- *Legal*: consumer law, employment law, antitrust law, copyright law, intellectual property law
- *Environmental*: natural resources, climate change, interest in sustainable business, pollution

The question is how does the organization handle the variety of mainly interdependent and sometimes contradictive factors? For sure, like in wildlife—where almost all animals are constantly carefully observing the surroundings—companies

© Springer International Publishing AG 2018
S. Hase, C. Busch, *The Quintessence of Sales*, Quintessence Series,
DOI 10.1007/978-3-319-61174-7_4

must be alert and keep an eye on almost every significant development. That means (a) what is significant? and (b) how much energy has to be put into this? One option is that the company does focus mainly on their core competence and filter only relevant news. Another option is that they do invest a lot of internal resources and knowledge to anticipate and accompany these in order to—in best case—influence and use it for their own purpose.

The answer is always a unique one. It is dependent on size and strength of the "animal" and its specific surroundings. Notable is that there are today in business not many "lions" and "elephants" anymore, which hardly have to care about their environment. Or to say from the business point of view: Even the formerly "untouchable" big global players have nowadays a lot to observe and to watch out.

Nobody knows how each single aspect will develop exactly and even less how the outcome of these various combinations will be. It is therefore more a general question in which direction it will go. Everybody agrees that digitalization will continue and influence more and more business areas. This means the environment is becoming still faster and even more unpredictable. Ismail, Malone, and van Geest (2014, p. 19) elaborate in their interesting approach on "exponential organizations" that "never in human history have we seen so many technologies moving at such a pace." They also claim in the subtitle that "new organizations are ten times better, faster and cheaper than yours."

As mentioned in Chap. 2, due to "big data" the available amount and processability of relevant data, and therefore the complexity, is already amazingly increasing. This makes every decision more demanding—for both the buying and the selling side.

So, how can companies deal with it and—even better—influence it for their business: Big players can found or join associations, committees, or councils in which they can communicate and aggregate their point of interests and at least create some remarkable noise. For the absolute majority of small and medium enterprises, these circumstances are however a given fact. What has to be taken into consideration by every company is the growing speed and increased transparency in terms of product cycles and communication.

This means:

- Life cycles of new products and services are significantly shortened.
- Less time to market the specific product or service and earn ROI.
- Investment in Research and Development increases as each company tries to launch competitive products, updates, or innovations.
- Competition is becoming more intense and much quicker in striking back with a similar "me-too" products.
- Blows and failures are communicated and "exploited" much faster by media and social media (e.g., "dieselgate").
- Awareness for "the next big thing" gives huge media attention and positive brand and product recognition.

In sum: Nobody can predict how the environment will develop—but big changes will occur. The complexity and transparency will dramatically rise, more information will be at hand (sometimes also a lot of fake and misleading news), and the speed of business will rise. This technical-driven development will not be turned back—such as "the black and white TV" will not come back either. Every company has to deal with it. It is—as it has always been—an important management decision, how to adjust the company to the ongoing change and to predict or to develop the next big trends. What is new is the accelerated time frame and the increased scope of scanning the environment.

Now, it is no longer sufficient to do a check in a 3- or even 5-year period of time but in a constant ongoing modus. And scope-wise, it is important to have a 360-degree view. Nowadays, competitors are no longer present in a certain and almost expected market segment only. For example, the biggest current thread for the automotive industry is coming from Google and Tesla– not from any of the established car manufacturers.

4.1 Four Forms of Structuring a Sales Organization

If the above is the given framework, what does this mean in particular for the sales organization? An organizational structure defines how employees' tasks are formally divided, grouped, and coordinated. It promotes certain behaviors and hinders others. In principle, any sales organization can be structured by its *products, channels, regions,* or *customers* (Homburg, Schäfer, & Schneider, 2002, for an overview). Sales organizations are usually not structured by a single criterion only. In practice, several criteria with different weighting and priorities are often applied in order to structure the sales organization.

In case of a *product*-structured sales organization (see Fig. 4.1), the departmentation is based on the types of goods and services of the company. The central advantage of the product-oriented structure is that sales staff stands out due to a high level of product expertise. As product specialists, they require relatively little technical support from headquarters and can solve customer questions and difficult technical problems on their own. A major drawback is, however, the lack of customer orientation. Sales reps who work in these structures are often product oriented and focus too much on product features. From our experience, they usually forget the consideration of customer needs and problems in their argumentation.

The *channel*-based sales organization is defined by various sales channels that serve the customers (see Fig. 4.2). The main advantage is that employees, who are responsible for a particular sales channel, have specific know-how about that channel. Particularly, with regard to the development of new distribution channels such as the Internet and call centers, this specialization can be very useful. The disadvantage of this form of sales organization is, however, that the customer contact across different sales channels is not viewed holistically. Channel representatives may also lack both product and customer know-how.

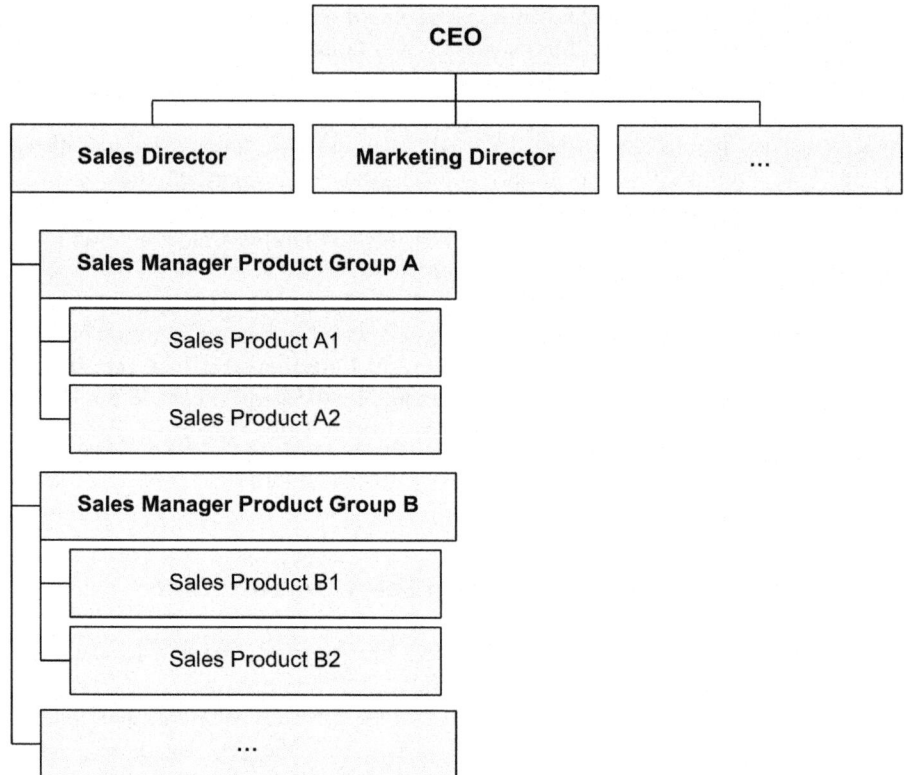

Fig. 4.1 Sales organization grouped by products

If a sales organization is structured by *region*, the departmentation is based on continents, countries, or regions within a country (see Fig. 4.3). The central advantage is obvious: There are often significant differences between different regions in terms of customer needs, purchasing behavior of customers, competitive situation, and general market environment. Additionally, cultural understanding and, not to forget, language will make a difference. In fact, region-oriented sales organizations secure the inclusion of these special features. They can also secure a "physical proximity" to customers. The disadvantage of region-oriented sales organizations often lies in their high degree of autonomy. Responsibility and decision making are usually settled in large parts in the regions themselves. In this way, powerful regional or country managers can build up counter-positions toward corporate headquarters. For example, regional market specificities are often overemphasized in order to secure one's own position. Another drawback is that market information from the region may not be completely or clearly communicated to headquarters. Also best practice examples are hardly shared between regions.

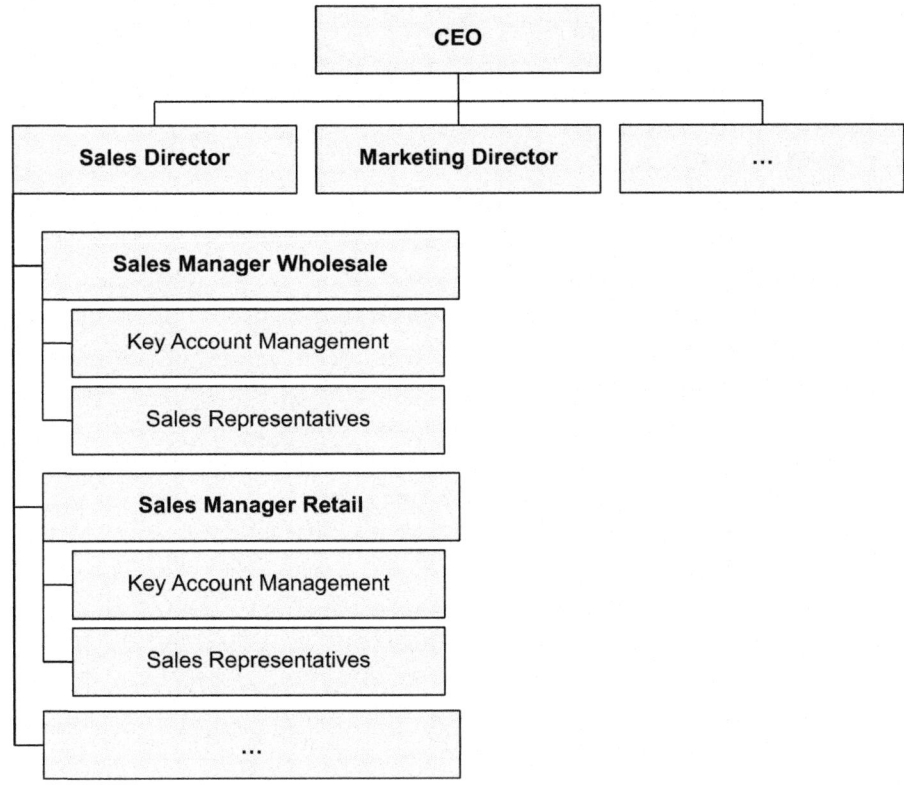

Fig. 4.2 Sales organization grouped by channels

Sales organizations, which are primarily structured by products, regions, or sales channels, can hardly cope with the increased demands of today's customers. The demand for qualified and comprehensive consulting services becomes increasingly important. A company that wants to convince its customers at this point must exactly know and understand the customer's needs and problems. This approach is best supported by the *customer*-oriented sales organization (see Fig. 4.4).

In case of customer specialization, the sales department of the organization is structured by the different types of customers it serves. This structure is completely oriented toward the customer and his problems and needs. Salespeople are "customer specialists," so to speak. They do not offer products *but* precisely fitting solutions that help the customer with solving his particular problem. The main advantage is that a customer-oriented structure can lead to a noticeable increase in customer satisfaction—and even customer profitability: Happy customers stay longer and buy more! A possible disadvantage is, however, that the product knowledge of customer specialists might be lower in comparison to product specialists. We believe that the benefits of the customer specialists outweigh the drawbacks. The disadvantages can be offset through appropriate structures. For

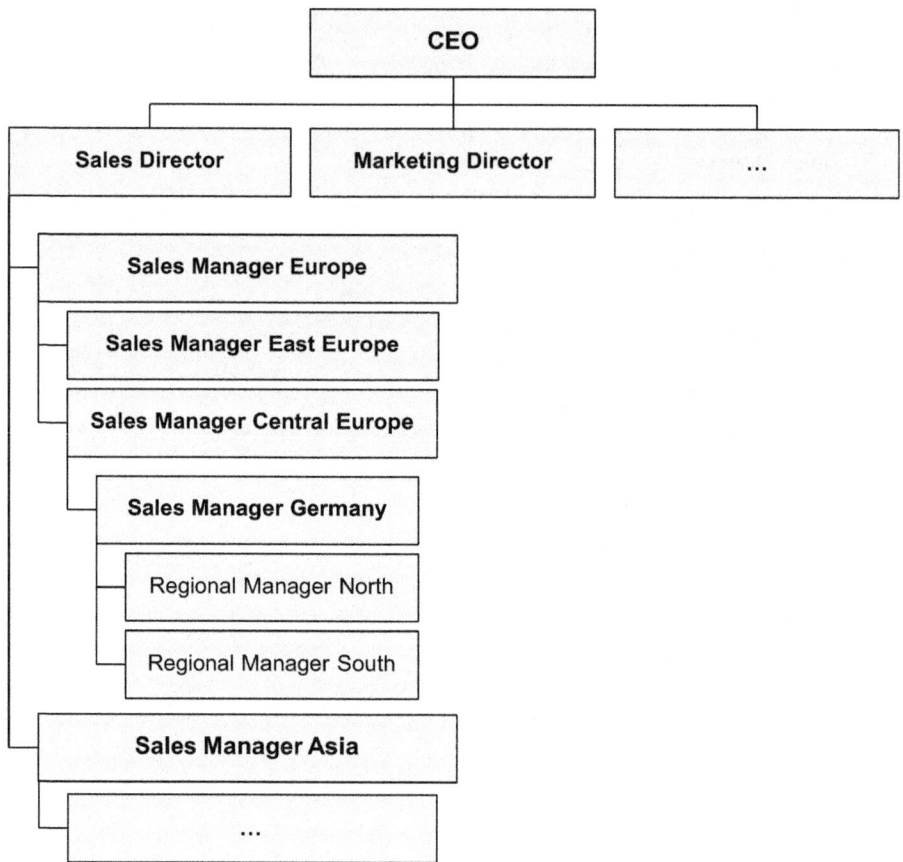

Fig. 4.3 Sales organization grouped by regions

example, salespeople and product specialists can work as a team, if necessary. In this case, the technical expert answers difficult questions whereas the sales rep is responsible for closing the deal.

Each of the above organizational forms has specific advantages and disadvantages. A general recommendation in favor of one form of sales organization is therefore not possible. We also think that general statements about "good" and "bad" sales organizational structures are problematic. Decisions on the organizational form always depend to a large extent on the characteristics of the company and the external surroundings. Based on our experience and observations, however, we can certainly say that many companies lay too little weight on the customer-oriented sales organization. In product-driven countries, such as Germany, the product-oriented sales organization still dominates. But in the face of increasingly demanding customers and a highly competitive market environment, it is more than ever necessary to put a stronger emphasis on a customer-oriented sales organization. A company must be inevitably oriented toward the customer.

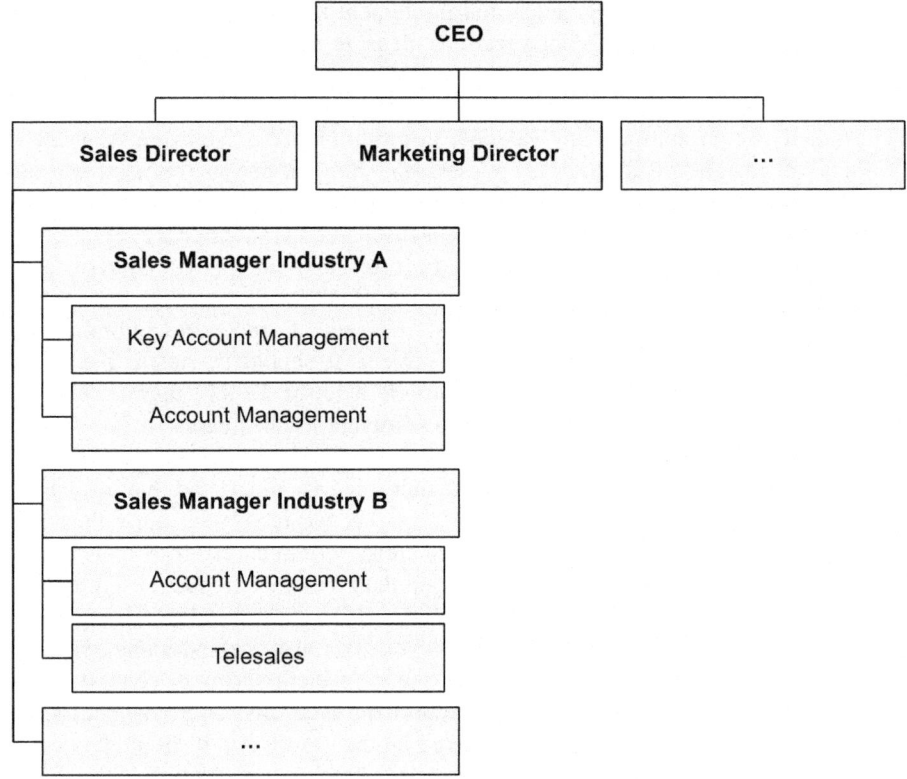

Fig. 4.4 Sales organization grouped by customers

Apart from developing the right organizational structure, we like to give three more general recommendations:

1. Companies should establish a professional *key account management (KAM) system* as quickly as possible—no matter how they have organized the company so far. In these uncertain times, it is almost a "must-have" that the most important customers are being served by the best available staff which should be KAMs (The profile of a KAM is discussed in Sect. 5.3.1). And not—as it is daily practice in many companies throughout the world—that "big shots" which are extremely vital for the ongoing future of the company are being handled by medium or even low talented staff. The reasons for this mismatch often lie in tradition, regional belongings, or time of company entry. We often accompany sales colleagues in the field who are aware that they cannot cope with the requirements of the big players. On the other hand, the big customers do recognize quickly that the proposed level of service is not the one which is being delivered. This is a clear weakness that has to be changed as soon as possible.

2. Companies should directly define and implement a *key performance indicator (KPI) system*. Today, many organizations measure one aspect mainly: contracts by margin or revenue. But like in professional sports, it is not enough anymore to have a look on the final result only. If you only know that the final soccer score is 0:0, then you do not have any valuable information about the game. You miss important insights regarding ball possession, shots on targets, corners, and so on. Hence, companies and therefore (sales) management have to analyze the sales performance professionally (which is discussed in more detail in Sect. 6.4). The classical "sales funnel" needs to be translated into a KPI system. For example, sales managers measure the number of cold calls (or other acquisition activities), number of initial meetings, amount of quotations, number of negotiations, and the sum of closed contracts. It should be noted that sales managers should not exaggerate and compile a set of 20 KPI figures. That is too sophisticated. 6–10 figures should be sufficient in most cases.

3. Companies should quickly install a lean but efficient *customer relationship management (CRM) system*. That means that it is easy to use and that it focuses on the relevant KPIs. Many CRM systems that we have seen are either too complex or too sophisticated. So it takes either too much effort to understand them or too much time to fill in all relevant data. Another frequent used tool in practice is a simple spreadsheet, e.g., Microsoft Excel®. It takes the opposite approach and is often easy to use. However, it is also a stand-alone solution which does not integrate data from the finance system and is in general rated poorly if it comes to targeted analysis. Apart from both ways: We have not found any CRM system yet which has been liked by the sales team. It should be noted that this is not the aim. The goal is to measure effectively whether the sales team is on track—while not hindering execution of their main task: Selling.

Besides these three factors from above, there is another important influencer: *Political power*. It is not only a question of which organizational system is the most effective one but also who is in charge and how to convince the reigning management that it is time for an update? In most companies, the first layer of decision makers are former product specialists or finance experts. Nowadays, there is rarely somebody from the selling side who is CEO or president. This is one explanation why sales is in most cases still seen as a "unit thinking" approach and not as a holistic approach.

Finally, it should be noted that—in order to transform companies into a more effective sales organization—it often requires a professional transformation without carving out "winners and losers" at the end.

4.2   Managing Interfaces

The largely embraced "customer orientation" construct emphasizes the critical role of effective interfaces within customer-oriented organizations (Biemans, Brenčič, & Malshe, 2010). Smoothly functioning interfaces in such sales organizations offer

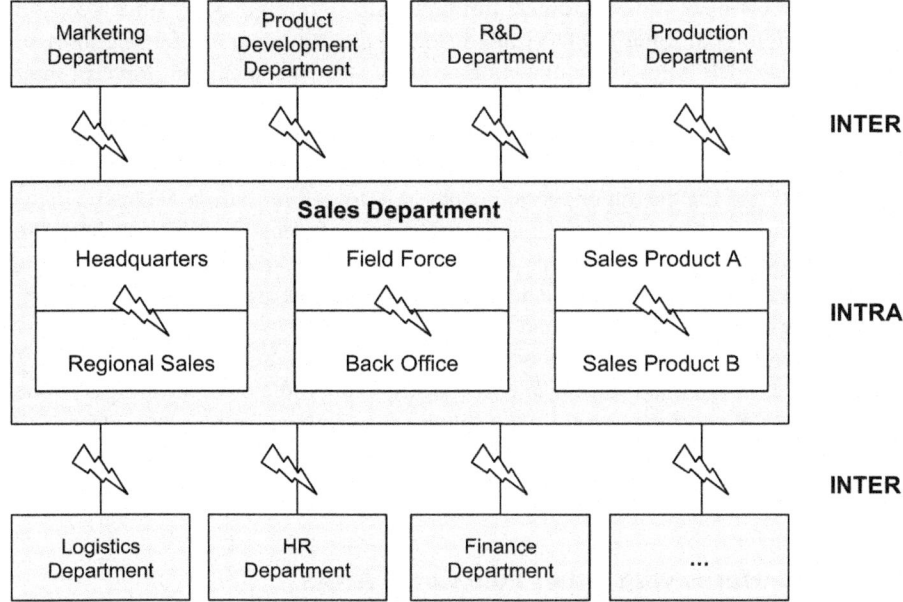

Fig. 4.5 Intra-functional interfaces within the sales department and inter-functional ones with other functional areas

many benefits such as fast market responsiveness, timely dissemination of market information, and the creation of superior customer value by efficiently coordinating the marketing activities.

The sales department has to actively manage many interfaces. Figure 4.5 shows the critical interfaces within the sales department (*intra-functional*) and interfaces with other functional areas (*inter-functional*). And it is as always: The weakest link here determines the performance of the whole chain. So the more complex the setup, the more internal communication and coordination is required. And the more political interests are involved, the more counterproductive battles are carried out.

4.2.1 Interfaces within Sales

The intra-functional interfaces within the sales department exist in many forms (see white part in Fig. 4.5). It includes exemplary:

- Interface between sales force and back office
- Interface between divisions that are responsible for different products
- Interface between headquarters and regional sales departments

Especially the interface between outside sales and back office is of great importance and a classical bottleneck. The field sales force maintains the personal contact with prospects and customers through visits, while the back office keeps in touch by phone and email. One problem that typically occurs is falling short of one's promise. The salesperson makes a promise—for instance, that the customer receives the contract in 2 days—and the inside service representative is not able to carry out the task on time. Another typical example is that a salesperson makes an agreement with the customer that he receives the delivery on Friday (in order to win the contract) and the customer service is not able to deliver before Monday.

A second typical issue that often arises is the lack of clear arrangements between the salesperson and inside service rep(s) and the poor quality of salesperson's records and documents (e.g., visit reports). However, the process of coordination is necessary to work effectively and efficiently.

A third problem that frequently occurs is the issue with "sovereignty over price." Often, it is observed that the field sales force still claims sole price sovereignty. The result is often an enormous need for coordination when back-office staff is forced to discuss prices with a customer. In this case, they constantly must ask the field sales force for competent consultation or advice.

4.2.2 Interfaces with Other Functional Areas

The sales department has also various interfaces with other functional areas. One of the classical inter-functional interfaces is the sales-marketing one. A company's business performance greatly depends on how these two functional areas work together [Guenzi and Troilo (2007); Smith, Gopalakrishna, and Chatterjee (2006)] as well as how well coordinated and conflict free this interface stays (Dewsnap & Jobber, 2000). Although both departments should work hand in hand and "speak the same language," we observe in many companies that the contrary is often the case. Hardened fronts, lack of information exchange, and arrogance are no exceptions. Marketers often think of salespeople that they only focus on their personal income bare of any relevant product knowledge. Salespeople, on the other hand, think that marketers are way off the market and do not understand the requirements of the "real world outside" and the motifs of the decision makers.

But not only the sales-marketing interface must run smoothly. All functional areas of a company must be geared to the high-margin marketing of products and services to fulfill today's demanding customer requirements. This also includes traditionally "sales-averse" functions such as product development, research and development, production, logistics, finance, administration, and HR. To achieve this goal, the interface between sales and the other functions must be managed systematically. We agree with Homburg et al. (2002) that interface problems that must be typically managed do include:

- Strong specialization of tasks
- Lack of information sharing between departments
- High dependence of departments in fulfillment of tasks
- Great cultural distance between departments
- Large spatial distance between departments

Fig. 4.6 Sales reps as relationship managers

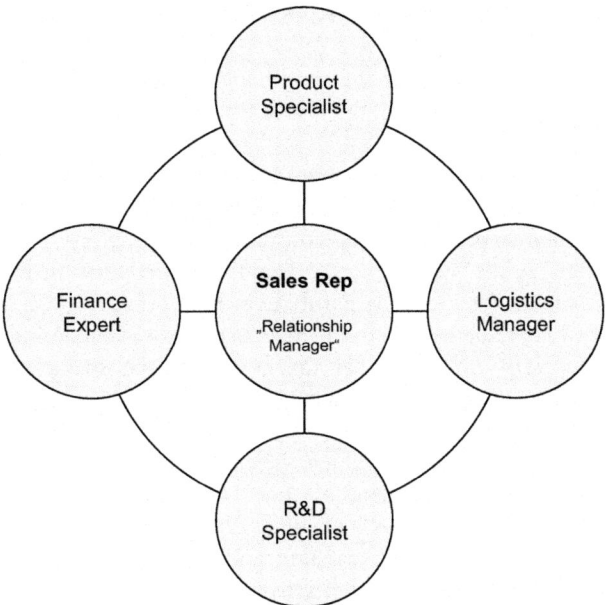

One instrument that can be used to encounter the strong specialization of tasks or to minimize coordination effort is building *cross-functional selling teams*. These teams include—besides salespeople—employees from product management, finance, logistics, market research, or other departments. Figure 4.6 shows an example of a cross-functional selling team. They are built on a project basis, for instance (1) for developing new products, (2) for selling complex product and service packages, and/or (3) for developing specific customer solutions. The teams are dissolved after the project has finished.

Due to increasing customer requirements and product complexity, these cross-functional selling teams are more and more necessary since an individual salesperson does not possess the knowledge or company-wide influence to propose and implement a customer solution. Thus, salespeople who are assigned to certain customers become relationship managers responsible for managing the activities of the team as shown in Fig. 4.6 (Weitz & Bradford, 1999).

In order to be successful, Weitz and Bradford (1999) suggest that "relationship managers" are able to build trust and interact with people in different functional areas and levels in both the buying and selling companies. They also possess creative problem-solving skills, conflict management skills, as well as planning and project management skills. Finally, they are able to work on and to lead teams.

4.3   Managing Ethics

"If money would be the only decisive parameter—then we would have all to be engaged in drug dealing" (Wendelin Wiedeking, former CEO of Porsche AG, own translation).

Every profession requires boundaries. Especially as sales has earned a partly shady reputation for mainly being ego and money driven. So, like in Formula 1 where "speed" is being confronted with "safety," the question in sales is how to align "profit" with "ethics"? That is how to define the moral frontiers of a successful business. This topic is hardly ever being discussed in sales circles and is not very well appreciated within the business, but it is becoming constantly more important. Especially nowadays, as the news and the social media spreads "fouls" much quicker and more obviously throughout the world (e.g., exploding battery of smart phones).

In a lot of big companies, the compliance department and others have developed guidelines how to handle ethics. Because the loss of an "ethical compass" can endanger the complete existence of corporations. Still the problem is that these guidelines are mainly created and communicated "top-down" so that the target group is often only very briefly involved.

Sales managers and salespeople are operating in a very complex environment marked by technological changes, shifting customer demands, strong competition, and heightened public scrutiny of company practices (Mulki, Jaramillo, & Locander, 2009). This situation can lead sales managers and salespeople to practice behaviors that are somehow dubious and questionable. These might even include "not really bad" behaviors:

- Misleading prospects and customers by leaving out important facts
- Exaggerating the benefits of a specific offering
- Making it difficult to invoke a service guarantee
- Using guilt tactics

Selling has long been linked to "sleazy" activities. But do salespeople still deserve this dubious place in society? We say loud and clear NO (although this question is not the point of this chapter). We like to offer advice that enables sales managers to avoid unethical selling practices but to build an ethical sales organization instead.

4.3.1   Ethical Challenges Facing Sales Managers and Salespeople

Salespeople are often perceived by the general public as having low ethical standards. It should be noted, however, that research does not support the popular belief that sales managers and salespeople are more likely to engage in unethical practices than others (Hair, Anderson, Mehta, & Babin, 2010). Misconduct can occur in all jobs and professions.

Sales managers typically face two sets of ethical dilemmas. The first set is embedded in their dealings with the sales force. We agree with Johnston and Marshall (2013) that ethical issues can arise in nearly all aspects of sales team management. Typical issues involve:

- Fairness and equal treatment of all employees
- Hiring of new sales recruits
- Promotion of employees
- Fairness in the design of sales territories
- Assignment of sales quotas
- Determination of compensation and incentive rewards
- Intra-organizational and inter-organizational behavior

A second set of ethical issues involve sales managers indirectly: It touches the interactions between the salespeople and their customers. A list of typical *unethical selling tactics and behaviors* is summarized in Table 4.1.

Although (sales) managers cannot always directly observe and control all actions of every salesperson, they have the responsibility to establish, communicate, and enforce *standards of ethical conduct*. This is of particular importance, as salespeople sometimes feel pressure to engage in actions that are necessary to close a sale. Uncertainty about what to do in these situations may lead to job stress, poor performance, or unsatisfied customers. Hence, the sales force needs explicit guidelines to resolve such issues (i.e., written policies). In return, salespeople can come to enjoy their job without the temptation to "just slightly'" cross the lines in order to win a certain deal.

When salespeople violate the standards of conduct, sales managers should discipline the employee in question. Of course, people may question whether setting and enforcing ethical standards for the sales force infringe on the freedom of its individual members. This is a great topic for philosophical debates. It must be clear, however, that ethical standards guide salespeople in dealing with their customers. Unethical selling practices may help the firm to make profits in the short run, but it will definitely not help in the mid or long run. It will only result in

Table 4.1   Potentially unethical behaviors by salespeople

1. Offer monetary bribe to buyer	7. Perform unnecessary services
2. Use of "psychological tricks" (e.g., guilt tactics)	8. Treat customers unfairly or rudely
3. False promises	9. Overcharge for services
4. Fear exploitation	10. Indirect material bribe to buyer
5. Create a false need for service	11. Hide mistakes or errors in service delivery
6. Sharing confidential customer information with third party	12. Cheat on bidding process

Source: Adapted from Dabholkar and Kellaris (1992), Schwepker and Hartline (2005)

the loss of sales, profits, as well as trust (!) over time and in paying remarkable penalties.

4.3.2   Unethical Behavior Due to Sales Quotas

For a sales quota to be effective, it must be (1) specific, (2) measurable, (3) assignable, (4) realistic, and (5) timely. Sales managers have to think about the acronym *SMART* (see Doran, 1981). Most decision makers argue that sales quotas should be set high. The argument is that salespeople are motivated to greater effort than without such a "carrot." The problem is, however, that high quotas can create ill will among the sales force. Pressure to reach goals can induce salespeople to engage in unethical or other undesirable behaviors. In a laboratory experiment, Schweitzer, Ordóñez, and Douma (2004) found that people with unmet goals were more likely to engage in unethical behavior than people who attempted to "do their best." This relationship also held for targets both with and without economic incentives. They also found that the relationship between goal setting and unethical behavior was particularly strong when people fell just short of reaching their targets. The use of very high sales quotas may be the exception rather than the rule nowadays, but it is important to be aware of this topic.

In addition, the use of high targets can lead sales managers and salespeople in a direction that is inconsistent with the customer-oriented selling approach. In one study of 316 sales and marketing executives, nearly 50% of managers suspect that their salespeople have lied on a sales call and nearly 75% believe that the drive to achieve their sales goals encourages salespeople to lose focus on customers' needs (Strout, 2002). Furthermore, the results suggest that sales quota can likewise drive sales managers to lose focus of ethical standards and customers' needs. When this happens, the sales force is likely to be less customer oriented. This will not foster long-term customer relationships.

We therefore do not recommend the use of overly aggressive quotas. The prevailing philosophy is that quotas should be realistic. Goals should represent a challenge, of course, but if they can be achieved with reasonable efforts, it seems to motivate most salespeople best. How to set targets for salespeople is explained in more detail in Sect. 6.4.5.

4.3.3   Creating an Ethical Work Climate

If the sales organizational strategy is to cultivate a customer-oriented climate over a long-lasting period of time through personnel selling, we agree with Schwepker and Good (2004) that there is a corresponding need to develop an ethical sales organization. The *ethical work climate* is the way in which employees view their work environment on moral dimensions. Babin, Boles, and Robin (2000) suggest that the marketing employees' ethical work climate is a multidimensional concept. It consists of four unique dimensions:

- *Trust and responsibility*: This dimension defines how far employees are trusted to behave in a responsible manner and are held personally responsible for their actions. A sales manager who supervises salespeople working in the field can increase trust by allowing the sales force to set their own schedules without constantly being monitored. Nevertheless, the freedom should be constantly accompanied by a sense of self-responsibility. If salespeople take advantage of their freedom (such as calling in sick when being well or intentionally misreporting one's work activities to the sales manager), they should be held responsible for their actions. Under conditions like this, the ethical climate develops positively.
- *Peer behavior*: This is the extent to which employees view other employees as having high moral standards. If salespeople observe other colleagues doing things that bother them from a moral standpoint, they will perceive the workplace as having a more negative ethical work climate. In fact, Cadogan, Lee, Tarkiainen, and Sundqvist (2009) found that sales teams are less likely to engage in unethical behavior when the teams have strong ethical standards.
- *Ethical norms*: The existence of policies, rules, and norms can also contribute to the ethical work climate. When sales managers and salespeople internalize the ethical rules and standards of the company as well as the boundaries for what is considered acceptable behavior, they are more likely to behave in an ethical manner (Schwepker & Hartline, 2005). They are often summarized in a company's code of ethics.
- *Selling practices*: As discussed, if salespeople feel pressured to prioritize "getting sales," it can motivate dubious or unethical behavior. When sales goals are unrealistic or overaggressive, closing the deal becomes more important than creating customer value by providing a product or service that perfectly suits the customers' needs.

Research shows that salespeople who work for a company that is known for having an ethical climate have lower stress, experience positive customer reactions (Mulki et al., 2009), are committed to service quality (Schwepker & Hartline, 2005), are more satisfied with their jobs, and have less intentions of leaving their present position (Pettijohn, Pettijohn, & Taylor, 2007).

4.3.4 Managing an Ethical Work Climate

Each of the four described dimensions can help to create a positive, healthy, and ethical work climate. Promoting an ethical work climate is the responsibility of management on all levels of the company. As indicated by Dickson, Smith, Grojean, and Ehrhart (2001), leadership behavior is the critical determinant of an ethical work climate. It is a *trickle-down effect*: If the top management is unconcerned about ethics in developing strategies, then sales managers are not likely to be concerned with the way that their sales force behaves. As a result, salespeople are likely to be unconcerned with the way that they treat their prospects and customers.

Accordingly, managing the ethical work climate should be a top priority for the management board.

Managers are considered to be a key source of guidance for ethical behavior (Brown, Treviño, & Harrison, 2005). Sales managers should therefore define clear boundaries of ethical behavior and advise their salespeople that they should not skate on thin ice when faced with ethical dilemmas. By communicating and enforcing the standards of ethical conduct, sales managers define the "operating space" and the lines which salespeople should not cross. This reduces uncertainty, increases effort, and ultimately improves job performance (Mulki et al., 2009).

The most effective way for sales managers to influence the ethical climate—and thus the ethical performance of their salespeople—is, however, "to lead by example." Sales managers who expect ethical behavior from their sales force should apply high ethical standards to their own actions and decisions. By "walking the talk" and by sticking to the rules and standards of ethical conduct, they signal to the sales force that the long-term impact of an ethical reputation far outweighs the short-term gain of getting customer orders through questionable means.

4.4   Developing a Sales-Driven Organization

There are, of course, plenty of ways to respond to the mentioned influence from "outside" in a competitive way. What narrows it down significantly is if the organization is committed to living up to their defined ethical standards.

Our recommendation for management that we like to offer is—what a surprise—a sales-related one. First of all, they should structure the whole company in a sales-driven way, so it becomes significantly more proactive, present, unique, autarchic, flexible, quicker, and therefore better prepared for upcoming changes. This is for sure not a guarantee for eternal or even long-term success but clearly for a much more successful coping strategy.

Out of our experience, a lot of companies struggle with the term *sales-driven organization*. Instead, they define themselves preferably as "innovative leaders," "trendsetters," "solution providers," and so on. Understandably, that applies more often and much better to the company's heritage, tradition, and comfort zone. But as discussed in Chap. 4: In these competitive times with its unpredictable developments, the main task is not only to design and develop appealing, sometimes even innovative, products and to wait for potential buyers who show interest and sometimes even purchase. Now, it is the time for proactively selling to them—in a high margin way.

Our suggestion is that not only the—comparably small—sales department is responsible for selling the products and services. If you analyze the headcounts in terms of full-time employees, it is often breathtaking: The sales department which sometimes counts 5—10 people per country is being made responsible for the revenue and margin success for over 1000 employees. That is neither a very logical ratio nor a solid risk management. In our understanding, it is much more effective, if the entire company is part of the sales process and is designed to fulfill this aim.

Table 4.2 11 Points for establishing a sales-driven organization

1. Creating a proactive mindset within the company	7. Upgrading existing interfaces to "high-speed mode"
2. Defining sales assistants	8. Making quick adjustments in case of underperformance
3. Adjusting the salary system	9. Spending more time with prospects and customers
4. Setting personal target agreements for everyone	10. Learning to welcome change as a driver
5. Conducting ongoing performance reviews	11. Strengthening internal personal communication
6. Matching best talents with most important customers	

4.5   11 Points for Establishing a Sales-Driven Organization

In the following section, we like to discuss the major milestones for establishing a sales-driven company. Table 4.2 provides an overview of the 11 points covered.

1. *Creating a proactive mindset within the company*: The essence of sales is to be proactive. Out of our long-time experience, the current situation of many companies is that—apart from the (hopefully hunter-minded) sales unit—the rest of the company is pretty reactive (so called "farming"). This is not surprising as this includes—apart from marketing—classical "sales-averse" departments such as IT, administration, technical support, human resources, and legal.

   If now every employee, no matter which unit he is working for, does understand the importance of his dynamic role and his straightforward mindset for the success of the whole company, then there will be a significant shift. By the way: Successful start-ups often have internalized this credo! Of course, it is more demanding to adjust the mindset within an established framework. And right, the bigger the organization, the more demanding it is. But it is doable.

   The amount of proactive opportunity seekers is then corresponding to the number of employees. (Of course, let's be fair; there will be some guys not joining the management's invitation. Nevertheless, it is then the top management decision how to handle those "preservers.") Hence, there will be plenty more chances in the sales funnel. The credo of each (sales) person should be: "I am able to initiate activities on my own. I can create ideas how to make the unit more productive. I am not only crossing my fingers and waiting for things to happen (e.g., incoming inquiries and orders)."

2. *Defining sales assistants*: Management should enlarge the sales force. If the environment becomes more complex, and if customer requirements become more demanding, then the management has to boost their front-line resources. Otherwise, it will be a "less" of everything: less time, less contact, and fewer

meetings with prospects and customers. And out of this—and this is the ongoing logic from Chap. 3—less sales and revenue.

So like famous Marshal Matt Dillon in "Dogde City" or Wil Kane in "High Noon," there needs to be more than only one to protect the city from evil and gambling (i.e., from changes, competition, and price wars in the business world). The task of an organization is to appoint and announce some more deputies.

As HR budgets are very often restrictive today, it is useful to take already existing roles and switch them into what we call "sales assistants." So for instance, technical support is not meant to be seen as a technical "troubleshooting" department only. They should rather be an additional business-oriented and sales-affine unit gaining further opportunities.

This requires first a new role definition of some positions in various departments. This could include technical support, in-house call center, recruiting specialists, and product training, among others. Second, it needs persuasive arguments to "load" the new assistants with knowledge, passion, and energy. Because only raising sales headcounts is just not enough. In addition, the task is to establish a good team spirit and boost self-esteem (i.e., "we are capable") of every single person. When the organization has created a general acceptance for a more proactive approach (see point 1), this nomination of new sales assistants is not being seen that critical anymore by affected departments.

3. *Adjusting the salary system*: Sales means that every single member of the organization takes responsibility for the company result. So every employee—again: no matter which unit he is working for—is no longer paid with a constant monthly income only. He should also receive an additional flexible salary component.

   It is not at all the idea at that stage to lower salaries. The aim is to make it obvious to every employee that their input has an effect on the whole organization and therefore on their wage. To gain some impact, a notable percentage should be shifted from fixed to flexible salary. As we discussed ethics before, it should not extend 10% of the income for sales-averse units at the beginning. For instance, 3%–5% would stress the idea behind it already and make it clear to every employee that he has to initiate actions to get the unit running.

4. *Setting personal target agreements for everyone*: So far, personal target agreements are mostly established for management and the sales team, but seldom for back-office staff or supporting units (e.g., human resources, admin). A target agreement makes clear how each employee can influence his flexible salary component and what performance is necessary to achieve 100% income or more. For every period of time, there are clear KPIs to guide each employee in terms of actions.

   Usually, the following should go without saying, but experience shows that it is important to emphasize this point: Targets are being discussed and agreed in a personal meeting (see Sect. 6.4.5 for more details on setting goals). Unfortunately, it is becoming pretty common nowadays that target agreements are not only being emailed to employees. It is also expected that these agreements are signed and returned in the same way without any personal communication. However, to achieve the important emotional buy-in from the employee and raise the individual commitment, every superior must talk with all his subordinates in person. The result will be a two-sided agreed and signed contract.

5. *Conducting ongoing performance reviews*: This is a classical weakness. Almost every organization has limited resources. After an introduction of a new idea, it is often a wishful thinking ("hope and pray") that the announced new approach will be accepted and lived by the team in their daily routine. Unfortunately, humans in general do not function that way. If the organization does not make clear its importance, then employees will readjust and return to their comfort zone. Hence, more management attention needs to be placed here.

   Biweekly, monthly, or quarterly review meetings between the manager and the (sales) employee have therefore to be conducted (see Sect. 6.4.1 for sales force performance evaluation). The time frame should be adjusted according to the importance of the unit and/or employee and his performance level. Sales means regular checking whether the train is still on track (such as the "time out" in professional sports). If reviews are postponed or not conducted anymore, the employee will not be aware of the relevance of the targets anymore.

6. *Matching best talents with most important customers*: If something is valuable, then companies should protect it the best they can. If something is fragile, then they should take care of it in the most professional way. Why do we mention this? Because it is amazing how many companies select only their second best employees for serving their biggest customers. There are often a lot of reasons for this internal mismatch: history, staff turnover, regional closeness, limited resources, cost cutting, and so on. To act in the interest of the company, sales managers should do themselves a favor and debug this issue as quickly as they can.

   Big companies have big expectations and—here comes another trend—are increasingly quicker unsatisfied. Tiny details do matter nowadays. Sales managers should therefore select their best team, if the "world cup" is being played. In order to get the process done, it is recommended that sales managers first define the most important customers as key accounts (so-called A-customers as described in Sect. 6.1.3) and then select the appropriate sales-people for the job. They also speak with the B-Team and make clear that this readjustment is good for everybody. If the company keeps big customers, it is much more convenient for everybody to work.

7. *Upgrading existing interfaces to "high-speed mode"*: The more complex the environment becomes, the more information gets lost on the way through different units and on its way to the prospect or customer. One classical organizational problem is that sales reps have incomplete information and suffer from available and competent knowledge. This leads very often to a lack of confidence at the point of sale and therefore to a bad closing rate.

To raise the performance of the company, it is required to manage and upgrade the existing interfaces. In times of the Internet dominance, everybody is expecting information to be available even quicker and more precise. Today, Google and Apple's Siri provide so much information that the organization has to keep up with the speed in order to be at least one step ahead of those "information competitors." Out of our experience, today it is not uncommon that customers know more than the sales rep who is visiting them (even if the meeting is for launching a completely new product!). But how does the company want to steer a process or communication if they are not in control of information leadership? This is especially true for providing relevant data about USPs, technical specs, and provided services.

For above reasons, it is of special interest to focus on the quality of the interfaces with marketing, technical service, and R&D (see Sect. 4.2.2). As this is also a political topic, it requires a common understanding in order to avoid the perceived feeling of losing grip.

8. *Making quick adjustments in case of underperformance*: What happens if performance is not on the agreed level? It means that the organization has to initiate actions in case of poor results. Not tomorrow, but as soon as possible, maybe even today. If this quick adjustment does not happen—in contradiction to the common target agreement (see point 4)—the whole system erodes. Many organizations are simply too slow.

At some time, they did develop a success formula. Otherwise, they would not be around anymore. But due to the natural enemy of "habits," they more or less try to hold on to that procedure. Minor face-lifting is pretty often taken as an answer to big challenges in the environment.

Please note: Reviewing results constantly and adjusting common agreements and actions to the achieved results does not explicitly mean that "another wave of change" is approaching. "Change" and "reorganization" have become real boo words for employees in recent years. Who wants to live forever in an intermediate status? The art of company culture for the future is to design a home-based feeling, which includes competitiveness and innovation combined with the accepted necessity to adopt quickly to market developments.

9. *Spending more time with prospects and customers*: All dedicated sales members (sales reps and what we called "sales assistants") should increase the "quality time" and the amount of appointments with their prospects and customers. The reason for being for every company—apart from nonprofit organizations—is to earn money. Sales members should therefore meet and speak to their target groups more regularly— and especially not only in the case of firefighting or troubleshooting. The latter case is a reactive mode. These visits are mainly being connected to problems, poor performance, or some pushing sales activities from the selling side.

So sales reps should switch the setup and make it a positive habit to meet and to call prospects and customers—it should not be an exception or emergency case. The same is true for sales assistants. If one speaks with employees of HR, administration, or other departments, it is surprising that these employees sometimes hardly know any customers in person. They do mainly communicate internally. How does the company achieve personal commitment, when the employees have never met the target group before? There are a lot of opportunities such as visiting fairs and attending speaker opportunities or summits.

10. *Learning to welcome change as a driver*: It is time and again astonishing how low the level of acceptance for new things was and still is. Following Plato's cave analogy humans are preservers. But due to external trends the logic remains: The more flexible the environment is, the more flexible the organization needs to be.

Good news: There is some light at the end of the tunnel: Nowadays, a lot of leading sport coaches (e.g., Joachim "Jogi" Löw and Pep Guardiola, among others) have developed with their teams an ability to play a variety of different gaming systems. So they are not limited any longer to a predictable game plan, but can compete much more effectively. This requires a specific core competence that was hardly before so prominent in sports— apart from chess: intelligence (sic!).

So learning and adapting is not something out of the ordinary but the rule! As no organization has the resources for permanent education, this requires for sure IT supported tools from now on (e.g., online academies, virtual classrooms, and webinars). And like mentioned in sports: Leaders who constantly educate their team and every single member do develop further and create a learning organization.

11. *Strengthening internal personal communication*: Teaming up is nothing new so far—so why highlight it? Because in many virtual driven companies today's communication is mainly being conducted via electronic devices: Skype conferences, webinars, exchanging dozens of emails, and so on. But if using mainly these channels, one forgets the important factor that real human meetings always have more facets than electronic ones.

As people buy from people—which is in fact an easy but great word of wisdom—then it is not only a guideline for strengthening the external communication but also the internal one. It is therefore recommended to create targeted events where the entire company (macro perspective) or team (micro perspective) meets each other, and where they can exchange and get motivation as well as new "innovative" ideas. Just some food for thought: this could be kick-offs, spring–summer–autumn–winter summits or academies, experience or innovation days, and special targeted forums, such as strategic business outlooks.

References

Babin, B. J., Boles, J. S., & Robin, D. P. (2000). Representing the perceived ethical work climate among marketing employees. *Journal of the Academy of Marketing Science, 28*(3), 345–358.

Biemans, W. G., Brenčič, M. M., & Malshe, A. (2010). Marketing-sales interface configurations in B2B firms. *Industrial Marketing Management, 39*(2), 183–194.

Brown, M. E., Treviño, L. K., & Harrison, D. A. (2005). Ethical leadership: A social learning perspective for construct development and testing. *Organizational Behavior and Human Decision Processes, 97*(2), 117–134.

Cadogan, J. W., Lee, N., Tarkiainen, A., & Sundqvist, S. (2009). Sales manager and sales team determinants of salesperson ethical behavior. *European Journal of Marketing, 43*(7/8), 907–937.

Dabholkar, P. A., & Kellaris, J. J. (1992). Toward understanding marketing students' ethical judgment of controversial personal selling practices. *Journal of Business Research, 24*(4), 313–329.

Dewsnap, B., & Jobber, D. (2000). The sales-marketing interface in consumer packaged goods companies: A conceptual framework. *Journal of Personal Selling and Sales Management, 20* (2), 109–119.

Dickson, M. W., Smith, D. B., Grojean, M. W., & Ehrhart, M. (2001). An organizational climate regarding ethics: The outcome of leader values and the practices that reflect them. *The Leadership Quarterly, 12*(2), 197–217.

Doran, G. T. (1981). There's a S.M.A.R.T. way to write management's goals and objectives. *Management Review, 70*(11), 35–36.

Guenzi, P., & Troilo, G. (2007). The joint contribution of marketing and sales to the creation of superior customer value. *Journal of Business Research, 60*(2), 98–107.

Hair, J. F., Anderson, R. E., Mehta, R., & Babin, B. J. (2010). *Sales management. Building customer relationships and partnerships.* Mason, OH: South Western Cengage Learning.

Homburg, C., Schäfer, C., & Schneider, J. (2002). *Sales Excellence. Vertriebsmanagement mit System* (2. Auflage ed.). Wiesbaden: Springer Gabler.

Ismail, S., Malone, M. S., & van Geest, Y. (2014). *Exponential organizations. Why new organizations are ten times better, faster and cheaper than yours (and what to do about it).* New York: Diversion Books.

Jobber, D., & Lancaster, G. (2012). *Selling and sales management* (9th ed.). Harlow: Pearson Education Limited.

Johnston, M. W., & Marshall, G. W. (2013). *Sales force management. Leadership, innovation, technology* (11th ed.). New York: Routledge.

Mulki, J. P., Jaramillo, J. F., & Locander, W. B. (2009). Critical role of leadership on ethical climate and salesperson behaviors. *Journal of Business Ethics, 86*, 125–141.

Pettijohn, C., Pettijohn, L., & Taylor, A. J. (2007). Salesperson perceptions of ethical behaviors: Their influence on job satisfaction and turnover intentions. *Journal of Business Ethics, 78*(4), 547–557.

Schweitzer, M. E., Ordóñez, L., & Douma, B. (2004). Goal setting as a motivator of unethical behavior. *Academy of Management Journal, 47*(3), 422–432.

Schwepker, C. H., & Good, D. J. (2004). Marketing control and sales force customer orientation. *Journal of Personal Selling and Sales Management, 24*(3), 167–179.

Schwepker, C. H., & Hartline, M. D. (2005). Managing the ethical climate of customer-contact service employees. *Journal of Service Research, 7*(4), 377–397.

Smith, T. M., Gopalakrishna, S., & Chatterjee, R. (2006). A three-stage model of integrated marketing communications. *Journal of Marketing Research, 43*(4), 564–579.

Strout, E. (2002). To tell the truth. *Sales and Marketing Management, 154*(7), 40–47.

Weitz, B. A., & Bradford, K. D. (1999). Personal selling and sales management: A relationship marketing perspective. *Academy of Marketing Science, 27*(2), 241–254.

The Sales Team

5

The time of loners is fading out. When starting a professional sales career in the 1990s, everyone in our sales team was almost completely responsible for his own business and track record. The market was growing, workloads and targets were achievable within a nine-to-five framework, and phone calls after leaving the office did not exist. Furthermore, our product cycle was about 2–3 years and real product innovation happened approximately every 5 years and was rather the exception than the rule. As a result, we had to learn the product setup only once and could then use it for years. Also customer contacts via phone or in person were well prepared but pretty limited. A daily hit rate of 5–8 contacts was already OK! And last but not least, response times required in general some days, which also counted for writing offers.

Nowadays, the speed and scope of business have increased with digital might. Email communication has atomized people's expectations for response times from weeks or days to hours and minutes. Over 100 incoming emails per day are for some of our clients' sales teams that we accompany "normal." And everybody is even expected to read and handle them—in addition to the daily business of course—before or after the "classical" sales time.

Today, product cycles last often only months and new product launches are quite ordinary in order to keep the own brand and its awareness rolling. What is really challenging for salespeople at that stage is that product ranges become more inconsistent. So there are less economies of scale in learning product knowledge. In addition, personal targets are raised significantly and, as a consequence thereof, the expected hit rate (like daily visits, meetings, or calls). Besides that, pricing has become much more flexible due to bundles, extras, and a lot of "specials."

Before salespeople get sentimental about the good old times and get distracted: In total, the framework has become much more demanding. But what has remained is still the same: The day has only 24 h... So, sales reps are at least at the edge where it becomes too much tasks for a "lonely wolf."

Of course, there are still some gifted talents who are able to decide a business or a deal mainly on their own. It is like in soccer: Lionel Messi and Christiano Ronaldo

© Springer International Publishing AG 2018
S. Hase, C. Busch, *The Quintessence of Sales*, Quintessence Series,
DOI 10.1007/978-3-319-61174-7_5

are more than outstanding players who often made the difference in recent years. But in the accelerating B2B world, this is more the classical exception than the rule. And even messieurs Messi and Ronaldo have—as far as we are informed—some quite talented teammates.

So, it is nowadays useful to involve some more players in order to shift tasks and to gain sustainable success. We like to give another comparison from the world of soccer: Spanish top coach Pep Guardiola is today always taking his entire five-strong team with him—no matter where he goes—because without a co-trainer, game analyst, talent manager, fitness coach, and agent, it is in his view not possible to change a team so quick in its manifold dimensions (WeltN24, 2013).

In the following sections, we like to elaborate the question: Who is a must-have in a winning team? And following the sports metaphor, there must be goalkeepers, defenders, midfielders, and strikers. And, first of all—top-down: a passionate and talented coach.

5.1   The Sales Director

Teams need to be build and to be led. Even if self-motivation is one required key ability in this field of profession, which will be discussed in Sect. 5.2.1, the sales director is one of the most important players. Because the more competitive and complex the framework is, the more details do matter. And the more a mastermind is required, who has the resources and competence to plan, to structure, and to bring every team member to the peak of his game. This includes the ability to coordinate different opinions, to support struggling team members, and to create one holistic approach as well as to "read" and comprehend inconsistent facts and to adjust own tactics.

Another important point: "The bigger the team, the more important the leader." One-man shows or even small groups (up to three people) may run very successful without a leader if each single person is really dedicated and skilled. But as soon as it becomes a bigger team, the internal social mechanism develops more complex and becomes more important. Hence, somebody has to be in charge of the team. Like Brian Tracy put it, the sales director has to be "a friend, a counselor, a confident, a stern taskmaster, and an efficient business-oriented executive, all at the same time" (Tracy, 2015, p. 3).

To assure the ongoing success of the sales team, sales directors are required to consciously monitor opportunities and activities, to provide a steady learning curve for employees and the organization, and to ensure internal know-how transfer. Having said the latter, salespeople—like many others—do focus in fact a lot on their own personal advantage. Due to that, there has to be a superior to define an efficient framework not only for a chosen few but for every team member (this also includes managing ethics as discussed in Sect. 4.3).

5.1.1   Qualities Needed

A study of Deeter-Schmelz, Goebel, and Kennedy (2008) asked 33 sales managers and 25 sales reps in in-depth interviews to identify the attributes of effective sales managers. The top ten success factors—with which we agree and which also count for sales directors—are:

- *Communication and listening skills*: Must be good in personal interaction and have empathy.
- *Human relations skills*: Likes to work with people. Does that in a natural and effective way and builds rapport with the team members.
- *Organization and time management skills*: Is able to organize and manage his own time and work activities.
- *Knowledge possession*: Has good knowledge about the industry, product, and business in general.
- *Coaching skills*: Takes over the function as a mentor and helps his team members to improve their (selling) skills.
- *Motivational skills*: Recognizes what motivates his sales force and rewards good performance accordingly.
- *Honest and ethical tendencies*: Is perceived to be truthful, straightforward, and ethical.
- *Selling skills*: Must have experience in selling. The selling techniques and skills —as discussed in Chap. 3—contribute to the sales force's perception of his credibility and thus his reputation. If sales directors do not possess these skills, they are not believable.
- *Leadership skills*: Is able to encourage and inspire his sales team. We will discuss this topic in more detail in Sect. 6.1.
- *Willingness to empower:* Allows his salespeople to take over responsibility and action.

5.1.2   Typical Performance Issues

Sales directors (in the following section, sales managers are addressed as well) have a difficult job and they are being criticized very often—either by top management because they struggle or fail to reach their goals and objectives or by the sales team who claim that he is too demanding. It is the typical "sandwich" role of middle management. Some reasons why sales directors may not show high performance have been summarized by Anderson, Dubinsky, and Mehta (1999). From our experience, these performance issues are still valid. They are summarized in Fig. 5.1. Let's take a closer look at each point.

Wrong Selection of Sales Directors An outstanding salesperson often gets rewarded by being promoted to sales management. However, a top salesperson does not necessarily make a good sales director, because the tasks and skills needed

Fig. 5.1 Typical
performance issues of sales
directors

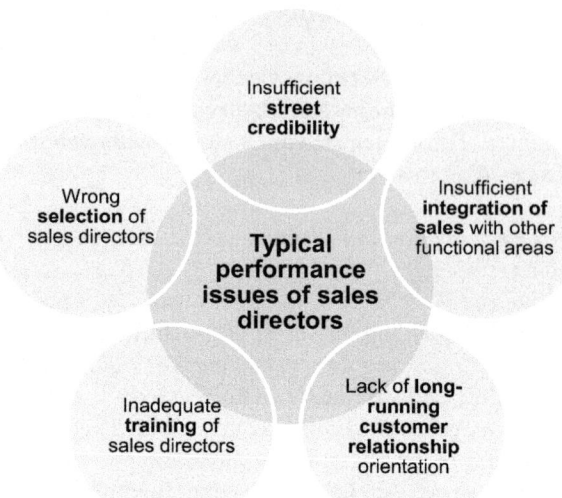

Insufficient
**street
credibility**

Wrong
selection of
sales directors

**Typical
performance
issues of sales
directors**

Insufficient
**integration of
sales** with other
functional areas

Inadequate
training of
sales directors

Lack of **long-
running
customer
relationship**
orientation

are generally different. Excellent salespeople often have an individual achievement need and want to accomplish personal goals and getting the results. Being first is great in their view. By contrast, successful sales directors must possess skills such as delegation and coaching in order to attain team goals. The selection of the wrong leader can lead to productivity declines, customer dissatisfaction, lower profits, loss of market share, and sales team morale and turnover problems. Sales organizations must therefore build a systematic process for matching the characteristics of the sales director candidate with the job requirements. The same counts obviously for sales manager candidates.

Inadequate Training of Sales Directors While many companies train their sales teams, they often fail to train their sales directors. This is of particular importance for new leaders who often suffer from role ambiguity. With adequate and sound training, however, sales directors can learn effective management practices. Also, if they learn how to pass on their newly gained experience and expertise to their subordinates in a way they can understand, the multiplying factor goes well beyond the direct target group of directors and managers. For instance, if a manager who is in charge of a team of six people gets trained to be just 3% more efficient, the overall gain for the company can be as much as 18%. Hence, management training makes sales directors capable of improving the productivity of their subordinates.

Lack of Long-Running Customer Relationship Orientation Some sales directors do not foster the development of long-run customer relationships. Often, sales directors, sales managers, and salespeople have a product orientation. They tend to focus on the product and the immediate sale, meaning that they emphasize their own needs, and not those of their customers. The consequence is, therefore, that the number of customers leaving the company is likely to be high. This will soon lead to lower sales profits and revenue. In contrast, if management focuses on the prospects and customer's needs and problems, they can develop a win-win situation which leads to long-term profitable relationships and mutually beneficial partnerships.

Insufficient Integration of Sales with Other Functional Areas It is necessary that the activities of the sales organization are well coordinated with the company's marketing strategy. Anderson et al. (1999, p. 23) describe the problem very well: "Too many managers think of … sales as an activity isolated from marketing planning and strategy development. It is not surprising that poor communication and even rivalry separate the headquarters marketing staff and the sales force in some companies. Instead they need to understand that they are on the same team and must cooperate to achieve organizational objectives." We totally agree with the authors that sales and marketing need to work together. We take it even a step further (as already discussed in Sect. 4.2): All functional areas of a company—including product development, research and development, production, logistics, finance, and administration—must be geared to the successful marketing of products and services. Only in this way will the company be able to fulfill today's demanding customer requirements. Hence, sales directors (and managers) must manage the interfaces with other functional areas.

Insufficient Street Credibility Apart from the suggestions made by Anderson et al. (1999), we noticed from our experience that some sales directors do not have the required "street credibility." The problem is that employees often follow the example of their superiors in the way they work. And the example they follow can be either good or bad. If sales directors do not "lead by example" (e.g., persuasive appearance, closing big deals), they will influence their sales team negatively. Even numerous appeals from the top management for salespeople "to work harder" and "perform better" lead to nothing. Employees only see this as a stick-in-the-mud attitude of their superiors. In sum, Sales leaders must "walk the talk."

5.1.3 Tasks and Responsibilities of a Sales Director

While the sales director's roles are constantly evolving when changing market conditions occur, they still center on traditional management tasks and responsibilities. Within the framework of organizational goals, the sales director's job is to plan, lead, and control the personal selling activities of his company. At the same time, they must continuously monitor and adapt to changes in the macro-environment. Like mentioned in Chap. 4, these external factors are often described by using the acronym PESTLE (i.e., Political, Economic, Socio-cultural, Techno-logical, Legal, and Environmental factors). As a result, sales directors (but also managers) have nowadays an increasingly challenging job that requires flexibility and ongoing learning. Let's take a short look on their tasks and responsibilities (see Fig. 5.2 for an overview). These are discussed in more detail in the following paragraph and in Chap. 6.

Fig. 5.2 Main tasks of a
sales director

Leading a Winning Sales Team The sales team needs someone who leads it—as in sports. Basketball coach John Wooden once said "Nothing will work unless you do." From our experience, the sales team needs a credible leader who among others:

• Inspires them to greater achievement by providing a strong vision for the future
• Communicates clearly, inspires, and enrolls his salespeople in his vision
• Has clarity in what he expects to achieve
• Instills a "winning" attitude throughout the team

The sales director is also challenged with responding to events within his team, company, and environment while striving for reaching organizational goals and continuously improving sales performance. Not an easy task—that is why we discuss the key leadership principles and tasks as well as how to build and develop a "winning sales team" in Sect. 6.1.

Training and Developing Sales Forces and Sales Assistants Developing sales training programs have become an important part of a sales director's job. In recent years, there has been a significant shift in the "balance of power" between sales-people and customers toward a buyers' market. Nowadays, prospects and customers are more knowledgeable than ever before, they get increasingly more demanding and have clearly developed ideas of what they are willing to pay. Moreover, they require individual solutions, and also products and services become even more complex and require much more explanation. As a result, sales directors must design training programs that help salespeople and sales assistants continually grow in knowledge, selling skills, attitude about selling, and customer understanding. How to develop effective sales training programs is outlined in Sect. 6.2.

Recruiting and Inducting the Right Sales Talents The best (sales) strategies are useless if there is nobody to professionally put them into practice and proactively live them out. The trouble is that good salespeople are like virtuoso musicians—they are a rare species and difficult to find. That is why nearly all sales organizations are searching desperately for that kind of people. And this "war for talents" will only intensify in future. Hence, sales directors must find suitable sales reps that are motivated in their everyday work and ideally fit in with the sales director, the sales team, and the company's culture. How to recruit and attract the right sales talents is discussed in Sect. 6.3.

And that is not all. Sales directors must also establish effective induction programs (also known as onboarding) for newly hired sales and experienced staff. This measure is necessary for new sales reps as it takes some time to learn the new job. During this period, the new recruit is probably unable to generate enough revenue "to earn" his salary. Moreover, staff turnover affects customer sales and retention. If an experienced salesperson leaves the company and his customer appreciated the business relationship with him, they may take their business elsewhere or follow him to the next company. Sales directors must therefore actively establish measures to help keeping talented salespeople on board. How to implement an effective induction program is also explained in Sect. 6.3.

Evaluating Salespeople Performance evaluation provides sales directors with a framework to manage their sales force. The appraisal process helps them:

- To determine training initiatives for salespeople
- To determine commission and bonuses for salespeople
- To make promotion decisions
- To motivate and influence employees
- Most importantly, to improve organizational profitability by improving sales force performance

It is for the above reasons that sales directors must (a) set targets of performance, (b) compare actual performance to the predetermined standard, and (c) take appropriate action to improve or to maintain performance. How to implement a successful salesperson performance evaluation is discussed in Sect. 6.4.

5.2 The Ideal Salesperson

One of the most often posed question that we have heard over the last decade is: "What makes a perfect salesperson?" Well, if it would be that easy to configurate an ideal sales expert like a car, then sales would not be the demanding profession that it is.

What makes this topic special is the logic and interaction we worked out in the previous chapters: The sales success of every individual is strongly related to the existing framework within the organization, the kind of external influences, and the character of the manager in charge. This setup is decisive besides the individual skills and attitudes of the person himself. Like in sports: If the coach changes, or if the play book is being adjusted, or if some new players are being hired, the performance of a player drops or rises immediately. And by the way: Even top players like Zlatan Ibrahimović faced that scenario and struggled at certain times in their career.

So to give a fruitful answer to the question above, it should be paraphrased: "What kind of salesperson is the right one for our particular company?" Or: "What are essential personal requirements for a successful salesperson nowadays?"

So, if (sales) managers ask an IT specialist how to make the network run, his answer will be that he needs a closer look into the various systems and interfaces. What we can offer right here is a definition of must-have abilities and a crucial mindset.

5.2.1 Overall Success Factors

Self-motivation is one of the keys to selling success (Rozell, Pettijohn, & Parker, 2006). Salespeople who have trouble with getting and staying motivated will not last very long. Sales is an occupation that is driven by *self*-motivation. The ideal salesperson is truly committed and has enough fire on his own. Those who do not achieve personal and organizational goals will be "weeded out" sooner or later by their lack of results. Many salespeople who believe that they cannot handle the pressure of selling leave the job on their own accord. In fact, salespeople must be able to handle the ups and downs of the business so that they do not get discouraged and give up. They must be goal oriented, always one step ahead, with the aim of winning new customers as well as keeping and developing current ones.

The other key is *empathy*. It is probably one of the most intensively studied personality traits in sales literature. Empathy refers to the ability of people to put themselves in the position of other people, to look at situations from the perspective of others, and to understand the problems and needs of other people. Salespeople with empathy take into account the perspective of the customer when selling a product. For example, they listen to the customer and build their arguments on a specific benefit the prospect is seeking rather than on a product feature. Empirical studies have demonstrated a positive correlation between empathy and sales success [i.e., Pilling and Eroglu (1994); McBane (1995)].

Based on these two personality traits, we can derive *four different kinds of salespeople* (Fig. 5.3):

Let's start bottom right and work through clockwise. The so-called *"coffee drinker"* owns a lot of empathy. This salesperson is listening to other people with a deep interest. He is genuinely trying to understand and show care for the person. Actually, this person is very good in developing an emotional level with a customer

Fig. 5.3 Four kinds of salespeople

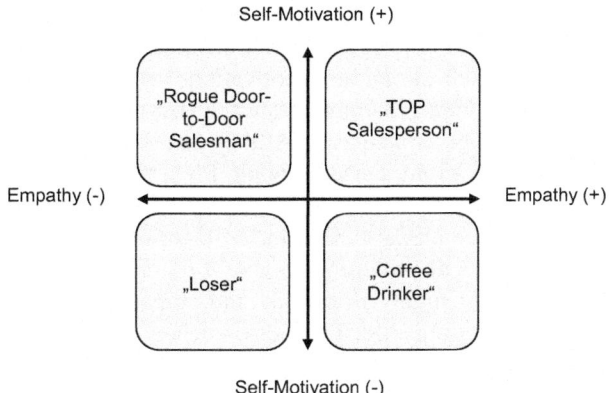

or prospect. What is missing is his straightforward attitude. He is a very good return player and has a clear deficit in initiating follow-up activities or even closing procedures. When he gets back from a customer's meeting and the sales manager asks about next steps, the "coffee drinker" might say: "It was a great meeting; we talked about anything and everything! And he will call us in a couple of months." This kind of salesperson is not goal oriented. A "coffee drinker" has not enough self-motivation to make the next step. And the next step. And so on. It should be noted that "coffee drinkers" are not "bad" salespeople in general. When acquiring new customers, they are actually good (team) players in the second row as they are able to literally "crack the nut" and to do the so-called "farming" (see DeCarlo & Lam, 2016 for more details). However, there are "better" salespeople as we will learn in a bit.

A salesperson who has neither empathy nor self-motivation is typically called a "*loser*" by our training attendees. This salesperson is neither flexible enough in coping with different kind of people nor is he oriented toward proactively closing the deal. Unfortunately, the result is that the "loser" is not achieving a good turnover. If sales managers employ this kind of salesperson, we recommend that the sales leader conducts an analysis of motivation (Sect. 6.1). If the salesperson does not work as the manager would like it, the person may *not want* to perform the job or task in question. If this is true, it is important to conduct a "motivational performance review" with him in order to clarify the causes of the motivation and demotivation (Sect. 6.4.5). Narrow leadership as well as the communication and implementation of consequences will then be necessary. It should be noted that those persons are not "bad" people at all and that they can be even quite useful technicians. But they are definitely not sales front liners.

Probably everybody of us has made already (bad) experience with the following salesperson—the so-called "*rogue door-to-door salesman*" (or hard-seller). Salespeople in this quadrant have a shady reputation. They actually do not have empathy at all: They do not care about customers, their needs, or wishes. The only thing that they care about is making money. They are highly self-motivated and sell everything—no matter, if the product or service suits the prospect's needs or not. Some of them act true to the motto: "Find 'em, fool 'em, forget 'em." Actually, some of these hard-selling people are very successful.

Due to their strong self-motivation, they are good in winning new customers which helps them to compensate the fact that they do a lot of "one-hit wonders" (i.e., only singular business). As they do not focus on an emotional chemistry, there is usually no strong personal bond. So in the end, that customer will probably not want to work with them again. Still, they are really successful in the so-called "hunting" (see DeCarlo & Lam, 2016 for more details).

Finally, we like to introduce the *"top salesperson,"* as we call this quadrant. This salesperson is highly motivated and empathetic. He is committed to selling and makes it part of his life. This person makes phone calls, initiates meetings, calls for a decision, and closes the sale. Everything is being done proactively toward achieving personal and company goals. And yes, it is entirely legitimate that top salespeople also do this work because they want to make good money. However, they sell not at any price. These salespeople have empathy with the prospect and customer. They build trust, they care and take their time, and they listen actively—with the aim of creating a customized offer that meets the concerns and problems of the customer. And if it does not fit the concept, the salesperson may also say "No, under these circumstances I can't help you this time." This makes the difference to the hard-seller and helps to create credibility and a stronger negotiation position in future. The top salesperson is interested in a long-run customer relationship. And he does that successfully.

5.2.2   Positive Attitude

We like to stress another important point that is closely connected to self-motivation: A *positive attitude*. The reason is obvious: If the salesperson's attitude is negative, he sees many obstacles and takes little or no action at all. However, if his attitude is positive and expectant, the sales rep sees opportunities and thinks the best of an idea, people, and situations. He takes actions to exploit the opportunities in order to reach a beneficial outcome such as making new appointments with prospects, negotiating good prices, or closing deals. Moreover, if a salesperson has a positive attitude, it preserves him—even in difficult situations—from questioning the success of a sale. Although a positive-minded sales rep hears many "No, thanks" and handles way more customer objections, he continues to believe in the success. This positive attitude helps him to handle negative experiences with customers much faster. This kind of salesperson shows great bouncebackability.

Many people think that having a positive attitude toward selling is an inherent attitude. Partly it is, yes. But: Many people resist the idea that a positive attitude is also a choice. Think about yourself when you were between 5 and 10 years old. What did you sell to your (grand) parents, friends, or other people? Maybe you sold lemonade or your old toys at a flea market or you exchanged stamps?! Think about your experiences at that time. As children—we did not think about selling. We just did it. We associated positive emotions with "selling" such as fun, curiosity, and success (i.e., How far can I go to get my way?!). If we look at it today, people usually have both positive and negative associations with selling. The reason for that is that we have all made our own experiences, for example:

- *Experience with other salespeople*: Pushy and sometimes dishonest call center agents who work with general guidelines
- *Experience as a salesperson with tough prospects or customers*: Hearing a "No, thanks, I am not interested" again. . . and again. . . and again can lead to frustration and demotivation
- *Negative influence of social environment*: Sales still has a negative reputation. People may say: "Yuck, how can you work in sales!? I would not do it for all the world!"

These and other experiences can unwittingly influence one's own attitude toward selling. However, it is one's own decision whether one remains a victim of circumstance or whether one wants to adopt a positive attitude and become a creator of opportunities. Attitudes can be changed and controlled. What it requires is to have the discipline and willpower. Making an inner change takes focus, discipline, and relentless practice. It is of great importance that salespeople work on their inner mindset. Not only the sales reps' outfit affects a prospect's attitude toward him but also his inner mindset—or "infit" as we call it in our sales trainings. A salesperson will only be successful in sales if he has the skills *and* the right attitude. Both are equally necessary.

5.2.3 Sales Abilities

Selling is not just "nice blah blah" as many people might think. It is a very demanding profession. A study of Marshall, Goebel, and Moncrief (2003) asked 215 sales managers to identify the skills, knowledge, and attributes required to be successful in selling. The top ten success factors—with which we agree—are:

- *Listening skills*: By active listening (e.g., nodding, giving verbal confirmation), the salesperson not only gives the customer a feeling that he listens with interest to him. He can also identify problems and pain points in order to build his arguments on a specific benefit.
- *Follow-up skills*: Yes, indeed! Salespeople always try to move the sale along to the next step of the selling process. The effort is devoted to the ongoing maintenance and management of the customer relationship.
- *Ability to adapt sales style from situation to situation*: As mentioned above, empathy is key. Salespeople must know how to handle different kinds of people—from number crunchers to technical experts.
- *Tenacity—sticking with a task*: The salesperson has a lot of staying power, for instance, if it comes to longer lead times or further decision rounds. He knows that it will take effort and hurdles to overcome.

- *Organizational skills*: Sales reps do not lose track even if it becomes complex or vague. They are multitasking, and respond on time, handle heavy workload, hold deadlines, and keep minutes. Visit reports are also updated.
- *Verbal communication skills*: The salesperson has good speaking abilities. He always communicates out of the customer's shoes instead of saying "We are... We have... We can....." He is also able to conduct a systematic needs assessment and offers solutions in clear benefit statements, as discussed in Chap. 3.
- *Proficiency in interacting with people at all levels within an organization*: Salespeople are able to deal with different hierarchy levels in a competent manner. If necessary, they can also deal with C-suite level clients (CEO, CFO, ...) or blue-collar workers. They have a convincing attitude in terms of verbal and nonverbal language. And most importantly, they radiate a positive attitude and confidence.
- *Demonstrated ability to overcome objections*: The work of a salesperson begins, when a prospect or customer says "No." Handling (acquisition and price) objections is therefore an elementary skill. It is nowadays for sure part of the game.
- *Personal planning and time management skills*: Only a few jobs require more self-management than face-to-face selling does. We devoted the next subchapter to this topic.
- *Closing skills*: It is part of the job to close deals with customers. Hence, a salesperson must be able to diminish last doubts and convince customers that they are making the right decision.

The key success factor relates to essential considerations. Sales directors and managers can use this knowledge (1) to provide a benchmark for recruitment efforts, (2) to give job applicants a heads-up on skills and abilities that are highly regarded, (3) to develop effective trainings measures, and (4) to evaluate the performance of the salesperson.

5.2.4 Time Management

Salespeople must be good *time managers* in order (1) to improve territory coverage, (2) increase efficiency, and (3) to maximize productivity. By having a good time management, they can maximize their resources interacting with prospects and customers.

As discussed by Hair, Anderson, Mehta, and Babin (2010), one way to be productive is *avoiding time traps* that can erode one's effectiveness. For example, sales reps can easily fall into this trap by calling unqualified or unprofitable prospects, by making poor use of waiting times, or by failing to prioritize one's work. Typical time traps are summarized in Table 5.1. It is best if sales reps have a system or procedure for planning in place in order to use their time effectively.

In order to be more productive, Hair et al. (2010) further suggest to *allocate time*. This means that salespeople decide on the principal tasks or activities that they must

Table 5.1 Typical time traps

Calling unqualified or unprofitable prospects	Making poor use of waiting times
Failing to prioritize one's work	Procrastinating on major projects
Making poor territorial routing	Making poor travel plans
Insufficient planning of daily tasks and activities	Doing tasks that could be delegated
Conducting unnecessary meetings, visits, calls	

complete. In the second step, they determine the amount of time they need for each task/activity. In order to determine how much time a salesperson is spending on each activity, it is useful to keep a log for several representative days—usually 1–2 weeks. Although they vary, typical plannable sales activities include making prospective calls, face-to-face selling, handling administrative work, making service calls, as well as traveling and waiting. After recording the times on an activity analysis sheet, the salesperson works with his manager to increase the amount of time spent on productive activities.

Setting daily, weekly, and monthly goals is a third way to increase productivity (Hair et al., 2010). Monthly goals set the target for number of prospective calls, number of face-to-face meetings, and type of customer coverage. The sales plan can set the course of action for the next 4 weeks as well as for the day. It is important to note that sales reps should plan their activities around the customer's time frame. Hence, non-selling activities, such as traveling, waiting, and handling administrative work—should be done during non-prime hours, whereas selling and servicing activities should be scheduled for time of the day when prospects and customers are available.

Sales reps should also identify the type of customer coverage. Ranking customers by the volume of business and profit generation enables them to focus on important accounts and to minimize time spent with relatively unimportant and unpromising accounts. The application of the ABC customer analysis, which divides the customers of a company into A, B, and C customers according to a relevant factor (e.g., turnover), is explained in Sect. 6.1.3.

5.2.5 Territorial Routing

Planning efficient routes that cover a territory is one of the most valuable tools in time management. Territorial routing is devising a travel plan when making sales calls. Sales reps develop a routing system or basic pattern by finding prospects and customers on a map and then identifying the optimal sequence and fastest route for visiting them. Properly designed routing system reduces travel time and selling costs and leads to improved territory coverage. The major disadvantage is, however, that routing reduces the salesperson's initiative and places him in a pattern that can become inflexible.

Routing is a difficult task for most sales reps, even if they are familiar with their territory. The extent to which companies use territorial routing usually depends on two aspects (Hair et al., 2010):

1. The *nature of the product*: If the product requires regular calls, servicing, and frequent meetings, routing is definitely needed.
2. The *nature of the job*: If the job is routine, routing is also necessary. However, situations that require a high-end sales force and strong selling techniques need a more flexible routing schedule. Fixed routing schedules restrict their ability to adapt to situations.

Territorial routing is recommended to all companies with a field sales force. However, flexibility should be taken into account when implementing it. Routing plans must structure sales calls that are flexible enough to allow salespeople to pursue previously unknown prospects. This is of particular importance if a company enters a new geographic area.

5.3   A Winning Sales Team

The effectiveness of the sales force is a critical success factor in meeting or exceeding company goals. There are four distinctive roles which are essential to cover when building a successful sales team (see Fig. 5.4 for an overview): The sales manager (in soccer: captain) is challenged with responding to events within the team, company, and environment while striving for continuously improving

Fig. 5.4 The four players

sales performance. The sales representative (midfielder) works on developing long-lasting and mutually beneficial customer relationships, whereas the key account manager (striker) serves a few customers with big economic potential. And finally, the back office (goalkeeper and defense) which makes sure that everything runs out smoothly in the background. The process of building and developing a "winning sales team" is outlined in Sect. 6.1.3. First of all, let's look at the four roles in more detail.

5.3.1   The Four Players

Sales Manager
The increasing (price) pressure on the market and the ever-growing demands of the customers and the company itself are daily felt by the *sales manager*. His activity has changed considerably. The requirements of management and employees rise and want to be processed efficiently—which makes this sandwich position more demanding. Hence, targets are revised upward, personally closing deals with customers becomes more important, and the induction period of new sales reps is shortened. Sales key figures, controlling, and information systems are becoming increasingly relevant.

A change takes also place in the personnel area. In recent years, the range of sales positions has increased significantly. Great salespeople are few and far between and these people are aware of their strong negotiation position. Therefore, new talents must be found and professionally integrated into the team. This gives rise to new demands on leadership—it is not easy to manage the balancing act between internal targets, existing resources, and different needs and wants of salespeople. On the basis of that, we suggest that sales managers have the following profile (Table 5.2).

Table 5.2   The profile of a sales manager

Sales manager		
Profile	• Is credible • Has a strong vision for the future • Communicates clearly, inspires, and enrolls others in their vision • Has clarity in what he expects to achieve • Instills a "winning" attitude throughout the team • Watches for (and quickly tries to reverse) team-building problems • Encourages positive, informal interactions between group members	
Dos	• "Walks the talk" • Is consequent in his decisions	• Justifies his statements
Dont's	• Only promotes best salesman (better: somebody who can also lead other people) • Loses trust of subordinates	• Does not want to lead people and to take responsibility • Is resentful

Sales Representative

Every company is paid by its customers. And as times are changing, they now in general expect greater value at lower prices while demanding better service. As a result, yesterday's sales reps who were characterized by a clear product orientation and straight— sometimes even manipulative—selling techniques and little interest in understanding customers' problems are out of time. As salespeople face diverse and sophisticated customers whose expectations continually rise, today's *sales representatives* must serve prospects and customers like a "relationship manager" or trusted consultant.

Today's sales reps stand out due to customer orientation. They listen and communicate meaningfully with prospects and customers, stress benefits and service, as well as try to solve problems. Their goal is to win new customers as well as to develop long-term and mutually beneficial relationships with existing ones. Hence, they must continually keep in touch with customer expectations, company goals, and changes in the market environment. Table 5.3 shows the profile of a good sales representative.

Key Account Manager (KAM)

Key account managers (KAMs) are assigned to the firm's most important customers—the so-called key accounts. These companies receive a "preferential treatment" due to their impressive current revenue with the company or due to their (cross-selling) potential. Hence, key account managers often belong to a small "elite unit" and massively affect the company's results with their actions.

They serve typically a very small number of accounts with high intensity. Their task is to develop special cross-product or cross-regional strategies and future projects for their customers. These activities usually happen several times per week or months and go far beyond regular sales activities. KAMs are the central point of contact and try to push the policy "one face to the customer." They therefore take a big responsibility on their shoulders.

Key account managers need a wider range of selling skills than the rest of the sales team as really big customers (e.g., with many company locations of lines of business) demand more sophisticated sales arguments than smaller accounts.

Table 5.3 The profile of a sales representative

Sales representative		
Profile	• Is actively engaged in targeted cold calling of prospects • Makes actively contact with decision makers and • Has regular personal contact with them • Knows his convincing "hooks" (What's in for me?) • Is empathic and strong in analyzing customer needs (pain points!) • Finds logical performance portfolio expansions	
Dos	• Is always one step ahead	• Communicates good business relationships: using references
Dont's	• Has a negative mindset • Is mainly reactive	• Is not prepared and structured

Their daily business includes the handling of committees and "heavyweight round," development of high-volume partnerships, targeted contact with top decision makers (C-level), strategic development and penetration of key customers, and the establishment to strategic partners. A derived KAM profile is found in Table 5.4.

Service and Back Office

A company can employ a great team of sales reps and KAMs. But this team will never be 100% successful if the back office is not performing well. The service team does not directly generate revenue for the business but provides a vital support and administration. They make sure that everything runs smoothly in the background, whether it is preparing documents and contracts or handling customer requests or complaints.

A number of key qualities are needed in the back office. In-house staff is characterized by having strong communication skills on the telephone, by showing empathy and an interest in people, and by dedication to service and support. A profile is shown in Table 5.5.

Table 5.4 The profile of a Key Account Manager (KAM)

Key Account Manager (KAM)		
Profile	• Is highly ambitious and goal oriented • Is able to handle complex matters • Loves BIG BUSINESS • Stays calm under pressure • Closes the chances in a competent manner ("hit rate") • Is persistent and thinks mid to long term • Communicates clearly and is able to lead a supporting team	
Dos	• Has a convincing attitude • Handles a group of decision makers (committees)	• Is strong in closing techniques • Price stability
Dont's	• Is overpromising • Gives discounts without reason	• Becomes arrogant

Table 5.5 The profile of the service and back office

Service and back office		
Profile	• Makes sure everything works 100% in the background • Works hand in hand with sales force • Prepares documents, contracts, and more • Handles customer complaints and requests on the phone • Continually improves the services further • Is flexible and enjoys daily routines • Handles heavy workloads (as they could often be a classical bottleneck)	
Dos	• Rings back every caller and • Answers every mail—quickly (!)	• Knows his sales arguments (being a sales assistant) • IT-affine
Dont's	• Only responds via email (better: calls customer back instead of writing an email)	• Is unfriendly, unreliable, … • Withholds information from customers and sales force

5.3.2   Key Factors of Successful Team Work

The importance of teamwork in sales increases; even virtual teams are no longer a rarity. But team work also means new challenges, both to the leader and to the members. The following key factors will tell sales managers what really matters in team work. The more successful the sales team will be:

- *Leadership*: The team needs someone who gives clear direction. Someone, who has the primary responsibility, who gives guidance, who answers questions, and so on. Leadership will be discussed in more detail in Sect. 6.1.
- *Goals*: A successful team needs also clear targets. It can only operate autonomously when all team members know what is to be achieved. Clear objectives avoid misunderstandings and give orientation. Goal setting is discussed in Sect. 6.4.3.
- *Tasks*: At least as important as clear goals are clear tasks. Successful team work requires good structures in place. It is recommended that the team leader clarifies who will take on which tasks. He should also make sure that everyone knows exactly what his tasks are and what expectations are associated with them. Ideally, the leader also ensures that all team members know how one's own work intertwines with that of other colleagues in order to work more effectively and efficiently.
- *Responsibility*: If each team member is responsible for fulfilling his tasks to reach a common goal, he should be therefore able to make the necessary decisions. Only in this way, the person can act to the best of his knowledge and belief. Out of this, the team leader should not only ensure that everyone knows what he has to do, but also specifies the members' scope of decision making. Each employee should know exactly how far his decision-making power and responsibility reaches.
- *Communication*: There is no team work without communication. No matter how well everyone accomplishes his own tasks and goals, the team is responsible as a whole for its results. Therefore, the sales manager needs to support the communication within the team. For instance, (1) by organizing *regular* meetings to discuss problems and progress (without talking endlessly!), (2) by fostering a positive atmosphere, and (3) by actively remedying misunderstandings and conflicts as quickly as possible.
- *Team spirit*: Nothing is more responsible for the success of a team than a good and trusting work environment, mutual help, and support. Binding a team together is therefore key. It is helpful if team members have a certain attitude, so that a true team culture—in addition to the existing company culture—can develop. Common values such as commitment, consideration, courtesy, give and take, openness, and willingness should be part of the team's self-understanding.

References

Anderson, R. E., Dubinsky, A. J., & Mehta, R. (1999). Sales managers: Marketing's best example of the Peter principle? *Business Horizons, 42*(1), 19–26.

DeCarlo, T. E., & Lam, S. K. (2016). Identifying effective hunters and farmers in the salesforce: a dispositional-situational framework. *Journal of the Academy of Marketing Science, 44*(4), 415–439.

Deeter-Schmelz, D. R., Goebel, D. J., & Kennedy, K. N. (2008). What are the characteristics of an effective sales manager? An exploratory study comparing salesperson and sales manager perspectives. *Journal of Personnel Selling and Sales Management, 28*(1), 7–20.

Hair, J. F., Anderson, R. E., Mehta, R., & Babin, B. J. (2010). *Sales management. Building customer relationships and partnerships*. Mason, OH: South Western Cengage Learning.

Marshall, G. W., Goebel, D. J., & Moncrief, W. C. (2003). Hiring for success at the buyer-seller interface. *Journal of Business Research, 56*(4), 247–255.

McBane, D. (1995). Empathy and the salesperson: A multidimensional perspective. *Psychology and Marketing, 12*(4), 349–371.

Pilling, B. K., & Eroglu, S. (1994). An empirical examination of the impact of salesperson empathy and professionalism and salability on retail buyers' evaluations. *Journal of Personal Selling and Sales Management, 14*(1), 55–58.

Rozell, E. J., Pettijohn, C. E., & Parker, R. S. (2006). Emotional intelligence and dispositional affectivity as predictors of performance in salespeople. *Journal of Marketing Theory and Practice, 14*(2), 113–124.

Tracy, B. (2015). *Sales management*. New York: American Management Association.

WeltN24 (2013). Mit diesem Team formt Guardiola die neuen Bayern. [online]. Accessed January 10, 2017, from https://www.welt.de/sport/fussball/bundesliga/fc-bayern-muenchen/arti cle117291152/Mit-diesem-Team-formt-Guardiola-die-neuen-Bayern.html

Sales Management

6

After having defined a clear sales process, discussed the importance of an appropriate organizational structure, and introduced the team components, this is now the final chapter. The showdown, which means: Mixing all presented ingredients—which can be pretty contrary in daily business—and transforming it into one holistic approach in order to gain maximum output. To use another picture: Steering the company sales-wise like a vessel especially in stormy weather.

Leadership and general management are quite popular topics. What is by far less touched is "sales management." But as it will be seen in the following sections, this group of themes is not a simple hybrid of sales and management tasks.

Besides: What is also been hardly focused on in the literature is—in our view—the general framework and guidelines sales management refers to. In a classical organizational approach, (top) management is acting according to the company vision. Out of this logic, sales management should follow the sales vision or at least a sales-oriented "spin-off" of the company vision (see Sect. 4.4 for the sales-driven organization—including ethics). This general orientation is mostly missing in daily business. Many companies today face at that point "terra incognita" and just install some stand-alone figures. However, e.g., "raise revenue, or margin, or xyz (insert most relevant KPI here) by x%" is not a dedicated sales vision but rather a fragmented goal and a short-term thinking approach.

Each task on its own—they will be described in the following sections—may be quite good to handle. Shooting a penalty in training with no spectators is something completely different, than doing the same in front of an audience of 29,546 people in an important final with live coverage. The same goes for sales management. When handling topics under time pressure, the track record of last quarters has been bad, motivation is poor, and the general economical setup is rough, then it makes every single action much tougher. Within a framework like this, it becomes, for example, significantly more demanding to conduct a review with a low performer.

Let's have a closer look on how to lead the sales-driven company.

© Springer International Publishing AG 2018
S. Hase, C. Busch, *The Quintessence of Sales*, Quintessence Series,
DOI 10.1007/978-3-319-61174-7_6

6.1   Leading a Winning Sales Team

Leading people as well as leading a team may always seem the same—no matter what background and profession the subordinates do have. But in fact, leading a sales team is already different than heading a marketing unit. It is like coaching a football or a basketball team. Again, we are discussing sales on a professional level, and here, it always goes: Details do matter.

Now, we take another step further: Leading a *winning* sales team. The more ambitious the team and the club—the more skilled the leader has to be. Coaching a club in a minor league is something different than coaching the national team. More people with big egos, more expectations, and more potential, which also means more frustration if it is not going according to individual plan. Hence, by raising the bar, it is plain to see: Leading a winning sales team is like coaching in football a Champions League club. And this is in fact a really interesting job.

6.1.1   Key Leadership Principles

There are many theories on how leaders influence their subordinates, including the trait, behavioral, and the contingency theory of leadership. While the trait and behavioral approaches focus primarily on the leader, contingency leadership theories place emphasis upon the interactions among the leader, subordinates, and situation-specific conditions. Far from these theoretical theories, we like to suggest a more practical approach. More specifically, in the following two chapters, we like to follow the pragmatic approach made by Fredmund Malik who is regarded as one of the internationally renowned experts on the practice of management.

Malik (2010, p. 80) states that principles are "the core of managerial effectiveness" and "the essence in any viable corporate culture." He has defined six principles of effective leadership, which lay the basis of professionalism in management (see Fig. 6.1 for an overview). They determine how (sales) leadership tasks should be executed. We agree with him and suggest that sales managers let their actions be guided by Malik's (2006) key principles irrespective of the personality traits or character of the leader:

1) *Focusing on results*: The thoughts and actions of competent sales directors and managers are oriented on results. This is what they are primarily interested in. At the end of the day, results are the decisive assessment factor for managers and their effectiveness—especially in sales organizations. From this it follows that sales leaders primarily support their employees in the achievement of objectives. This also means that sales leaders must carry out tasks that do not make "fun". For instance, decisions must be made which can be unpleasant.
2) *Contribution to the whole*: Of course, the results achieved must be related to the purpose of the organization. The more specialization and the greater the division of labor, the higher the risk that people lose the sense of purpose. For that reason,

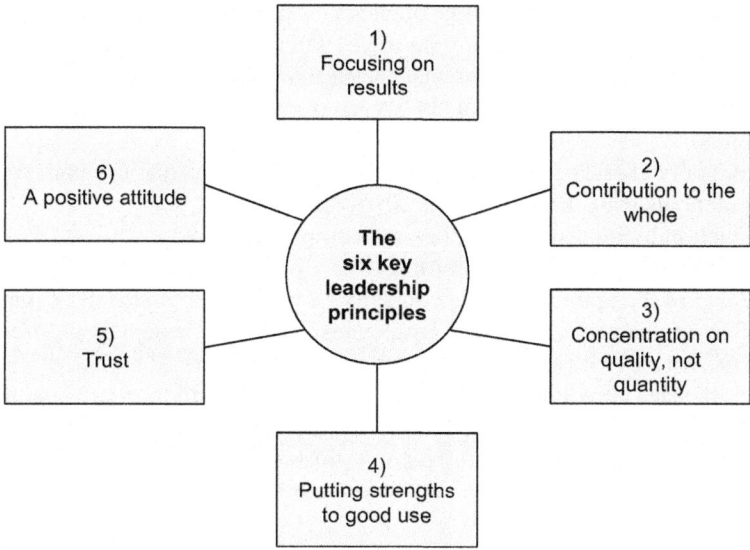

Fig. 6.1   The six key leadership principles

sales directors and managers must be clear about their substantial contribution to the whole.

In accordance with the above, we suggest that leaders answer the following questions:

- What are the business objectives of my division/team?
- What are the five main activities of my team?
- What development potentials has my team?
- What is my own/my team's contribution to the whole?
- Who benefits from what my team is doing (i.e., customers, departments, employees)?

3) *Concentration on quality, not quantity*: As the idiom says, "less is more"! Managers often do too many tasks and projects at the same time. However, only by concentrating and focusing on a small number of carefully selected focal points, they can achieve real impact and success. And exactly this is the task of an organization: It has been composed to achieve a common goal or a set of goals. Hence, it is all about achieving performance and attaining results.

Having said the above, we suggest that sales leaders ask themselves the following questions:

- What do I primarily want to achieve within the next x months?
- What are my three focal points within the next x months?
- What are my most important operative tasks?
- How can I achieve enough capacity for effective leadership?
- How do I organize my work goal oriented and effectively?

4) *Putting strengths to good use*: Managers often focus on their employee's weaknesses rather than focusing on their strengths. However, performance can only be expected to the extent that the design of tasks permits employees to deliver their contributions exactly where they have their natural talents and strengths.

From our experience, we recommend that sales leaders identify both strengths and potentials of their team and its single members:

- Which individual strengths does each employee have?
- Are these strengths used accordingly?
- What are the options that the company can use the strengths even more?
- What are the potentials of the employees? Who can be deployed differently?
- What core weaknesses must be made meaningless?

5) *Trust*: If sales directors and managers succeed in building and maintaining trustful relationships, then their authority will be robust and reliable. If trust has been established, it can cushion mistakes. Both sales manager and employees know that they can rely on each other. Malik (2006) lists effective rules for building trust:

- Looking from the outside and top-down, errors of the employee are errors of the manager. When looking from the inside, errors must be dealt with by constructive feedback and punishments (if needed).
- Errors of the manager are errors of the sales manager—without exception.
- Successes of an employee belong to the employee. Managers do not adorn themselves with borrowed plumes.
- Successes of the manager are successes of the team, if they are good managers. Rather than claiming the achievement for themselves, they say: "*We* did it."

6) *A positive attitude*: Good managers think positively and constructively. They always give their best and do not complain about *how* it is. They know that a negative attitude will stand in their way of success. Instead of focusing their attention on the problem, they look for chances and opportunities behind it. Of course, this view is not always easy, but the probability to find a solution for the problem at hand is much higher. So this positive attitude alone is a competitive advantage.

6.1.2 Key Leadership Tasks

We will now have a closer look on the various sales manager's leadership tasks. In accordance with Malik (2006), we suggest that sales directors and managers need to focus on five tasks to be effective in their role:

1) *Managing objectives*: The first task of effective management is to ensure that targets are set. These need to be the right goals and they need to be clear. A management by objectives (MBO) program can be invaluable at this stage. In this regard, the sales manager and the individual salesperson jointly agree on the

sales reps' specific goals or performance targets for the coming period. The MBO cycle is discussed in Sect. 6.4.3. Targets are the means to focus the organization. They also exert a decisive influence on the effectiveness of people—goals enable us to instill meaning and purpose into everything we do (Tracy, 2010).

Questions that sales leaders need to ask themselves include in our view:

- What are the specific objectives for my team and for each single employee?
- How do I communicate the goals?
- How do I support the work processes?
- What are the current "bottlenecks" and "hurdles" in the achievement of objectives?

2) *Organizing*: Leaders need to ensure that employees are working on what the customer pays for. The entire company, not just the sales department, needs to be set up in a way that all employees can contribute their skills to the whole.

Having said the above, we suggest that sales managers ask themselves:

- Does every employee have a clearly defined task?
- Does each employee understand the management's expectations?
- Are work processes explicitly directed toward the achievement of objectives?
- Are there rules of cooperation (inter- and intra-functional)?

3) *Decision making*: Deciding is the core nature of leadership. It is the most critical management task—"the task which makes or breaks the manager" (Malik, 2006, p. 180). The decision-making process does not only include the precise specification of the problem, it also contains working out alternatives, analyzing risks, consequences, and boundary conditions of each alternative, and making a final decision. Effective managers also implement their decisions and place great value on the follow-up and follow-through. This makes sure that the important things are really done (Malik, 2011).

We recommend in that context that sales managers ask themselves the following questions:

- Who makes decisions on which level?
- How are decisions communicated?
- Who makes decisions for the interfaces?
- How consistent are decisions implemented?

4) *Supervising*: The work of each salesperson has to be measured and controlled so that the desired performance can be delivered. Where it is not possible to measure, contributions have to be assessed and judged.

Questions that sales managers need to ask themselves include in our view:

- How often should performance appraisals take place?
- How are the results regularly controlled?
- What happens when results are outstanding?
- What happens when unsatisfactory results occur?

5) *Developing people*: Employees are the most important part of an organization. Hence, it is a prime responsibility of the sales manager to develop his sales force—knowing them and placing them where they can contribute their strength and where their weakness becomes less important (discussed later).

From our experience, questions that sales managers need to ask themselves include:
- How do I support my high and low performers?
- What challenging projects can I offer high performers?
- What are the causes for low performance (see Sect. 6.1.3 for analysis of motivation)?
- What concrete consequences can low performers expect?

Malik's (2006) approach is a very task-focused description of management. It breaks down the areas of responsibility and steps and has become the standard approach in many European organizations. On that basis, we have developed an assessment sheet, in which sales directors and managers can reflect on how effectively they carried out the five leadership tasks (Fig. 6.2).

6.1.3 Building and Developing a Winning Sales Team

Managers affect the motivation of their employees as well as their work objectives and role clarity in a crucial way. Especially in sales, significant productivity problems may occur. As a result: What are key leadership behaviors to form a productive sales team? Many sales leaders are looking for an answer to this question. Hence, research on leadership theory has been voluminous over the past three decades. Some of the ways to understand leadership include individual traits, behaviors, role relationships, and interaction patterns (Yukl, 2006). Far from the many theoretical approaches, we like to suggest a more practical approach. The process of building and developing a winning sales team is outlined in Fig. 6.3.

1) Analyze Exactly Your Sales Team
The first step in developing a winning sales team is to conduct an analysis of the existing sales force. Sales managers review exactly each member of the team to identify their personal strengths and development potentials (we do not like the term "weaknesses") in terms of his inner mindset, knowledge, and selling abilities. A common typology that has proven itself in practice contains three areas of competencies:

- *Technical competence*: Technical knowledge and specific experience, e.g., company knowledge, product and service knowledge, and market and customer knowledge
- *Methodical competence*: Ability to find solutions through targeted procedures, e.g., conducting conversations, presentation skills
- *Social competence*: Ability for teamwork and productive communication, i.e., contact with clients and interested parties; emotional capability; self-motivation

ASSESSMENT SHEET (Excerpt)

Key leadership tasks – Rating others or oneself

Please rate the performance of the leader in question:

	+	o	-	Comments
Managing objectives				
Communicates behavioral expectations to employees				
Acts consistently				
Achieves targets even under difficult conditions				
Agrees on common goals				
Organizing				
Has effectively developed structures				
Has good organization and time management				
Adaptation of the organization to customer needs				
Monitors process, progress, and results				
Decision-making				
Develops alternatives				
Third parties are involved in decision-making				
Communicates decisions consistently				
Supports the implementation of decisions				
Supervising				
Has basically a trusting attitude towards employees				
Communicates openly critical things				
Assessment is based on results				
Promotes constructive feedback				
Takes consequences for misconduct / low performance				
Developing people				
Gives employees challenging tasks				
Actively promotes motivation of employees				
Works consistently on the strengths of employees				
Reduces systematically the weaknesses of employees				

Fig. 6.2 Assessment sheet—key leadership tasks (Excerpt)

Various instruments can be used for the evaluation: By *field accompaniments*—probably the most effective way—the sales manager or trainer accompanies each salesperson in the field. The employee usually schedules 2–3 appointments with customers and/or prospects or makes a fixed number of calls within 1 day. In between of the activities, both analyze the performance. By doing so, the sales

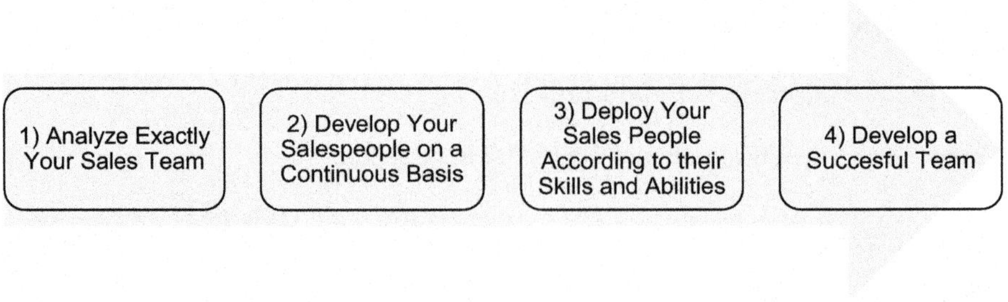

1) Analyze Exactly Your Sales Team	2) Develop Your Salespeople on a Continuous Basis	3) Deploy Your Sales People According to their Skills and Abilities	4) Develop a Succesful Team

Fig. 6.3 Process of building a winning sales team

manager can evaluate the personal strengths and development potentials in relation to the essential skills.

Alternatively—or in addition to field accompaniments—sales managers can conduct *structured interviews* with each subordinate. This approach does not only help to get a good understanding of the subordinate's knowledge and attitude toward sales. It may even be essential for a proper understanding of the company's most unique selling points and key challenges in the sales process for the coming years. Interview questions may include:

• What do you associate with the term "customer acquisition"?
• How well do you think you take care of your customers/prospects?
• How would you summarize the "secret" of our company's success in one sentence?
• What particular growth opportunities do you see?

To analyze salespeople, managers can also use *reporting systems* and *performance appraisals* as discussed in Sect. 6.4. After having decided what instrument is used, the sales manager evaluates each team member in written form as shown in Table 6.1.

Application questions for sales managers:

1. *On a scale from 1 to 10, how good do you know your people?*
2. *What instruments will you use to gain a (more) holistic picture of each team member?*
3. *What are the team member's strengths and development potentials?*

Table 6.1 Employee evaluation—subordinate #1

Strengths	Development potentials
• Convincing attitude • Strong in building an emotional bond with new contacts • Speaking abilities • . . .	• Structure in conversational talks • Analyzing customer needs (pain points) • Closing techniques • . . .

2) Develop Your Salespeople on a Continuous Basis

Based on the analysis, the sales manager develops the sales force on a continuous basis. An appreciated side effect of this measure is that getting a more demanding task is often considered an honor and a sign of recognition. Typical developmental measures to choose from in sales organizations include:

- *Mentoring systems*: A practically proven way to develop salespeople and leaders is through mentoring. A mentor is typically an older, more experienced person who systematically helps develop a subordinate's or colleague's abilities. Mentors usually provide career-related support (e.g., sponsorship, coaching, challenging assignments) and psychosocial support (e.g., friendship, counseling, role modeling) (Kram, 1985). Sales managers, and also high-performing sales reps, are an important source for the development of salespeople.
- *"Curbstone coaching"*: Another form that has recently gained popularity among sales managers is "curbstone coaching" (Hair, Anderson, Mehta, & Babin, 2010). The sales manager or an external trainer and the subordinate go to several customer meetings. On the way to the next appointment, the manager provides a constructive feedback and solid information on "how to do better" next time. The sales manager himself may also want to take the lead in the next customer meeting. In this way, the salesperson can observe his sales manager practicing what he preaches. This is in line with Bandura (1986) who posits that individuals learn what to do and how to behave largely by observing and emulating role models.
- *Special tasks in the team member's own area*: Sales managers give salespeople special projects (e.g., induction of new sales reps; development of sales plan) with respect to their knowledge, experience, and internal motivation. In this way, sales reps can improve their strengths even more.
- *Temporary delegation of responsibilities*: The idea behind this is the concept of empowerment which focuses on the delegation of decision-making authority and responsibility from managers to lower-level employees (Ford & Fottler, 1995). Delegating responsibility to sales reps has two distinct advantages. First, the good old excuse that "I'm just supposed to do what my superior tells me and not more" is no longer viable. Second, empowerment can help improve self-efficacy and alleviate powerlessness of employees—especially of high-performing sales reps who want to rise the career ladder.

Table 6.2 Action plan—subordinate #1

What is the developmental measure?	What is the subordinate's (possible) reaction?	Who is involved in the measure?	Until when is the measure being implemented?
Curbstone coaching: 2–3 customer meetings in 1 day	Rejection and fear Being cautious	External trainer	dd/mm/yyyy
. . .	. . .	. . .	. . .

The sales manager develops a list of possible developmental measures for each subordinate. Before discussing the action plan with the salesperson, it is important to think about the subordinate's possible reaction to the entire measure. In this way, the sales manager can react appropriately to upcoming excuses, concerns, fears, and questions. In addition, the sales leader should decide who is involved in the development measure. This person may be the sales manager himself, an external trainer, or other colleagues. High performers, for instance, who need to get a more challenging task, can be used for developing new or inexperienced sales reps and low performers through mentoring or "curbstone coaching." Finally, a deadline for implementation should be set. An action plan is summarized in Table 6.2 which lays the foundation for the conversation with the subordinate(s).

Application questions for sales managers:

1. *What precise areas of improvement do you identify to develop each of your subordinates?*
2. *What opportunities are given to high performers? How do you develop them systematically?*
3. *What is the best action plan for each subordinate?*

3) Deploy Your Salespeople According to their Skills and Abilities

As discussed above, managers often focus on their employee's weaknesses rather than on their strengths. However, performance can only be expected to the extent that the design of tasks permits employees to deliver their contributions exactly where they have their natural talents and strengths. If this is the case, peak performance will suddenly be achieved and the problems of demotivation will disappear. We therefore suggest that sales managers *use the existing strengths and potentials of their team members*. Sales reps who have strong analytical skills and a structured approach to problem-solving may be very strong in analyzing customer needs and pain points. However, these people may lack some of the key skills and abilities—such as flexibility and persuasive power—required to success-fully close the deal.

It is for the above reason that numerous companies apply the *ABC (customer)
analysis* which divides the customers of a company into A, B, and C categories. The
A group represents only 20% of all customers but generates 80% of the sales
volume. Group B and C are responsible for the remaining 20%. In key account
management, the ABC analysis is the most applied approach in selecting key or
major accounts (Wengler, Ehret, & Saab, 2006). In this case, the team comprises
senior salespeople who specialize in dealing with large customers who demand
more sophisticated sales arguments and different decision-making processes than
smaller companies. The range of selling skills required is therefore wider than for
the rest of the sales team, who deal with smaller accounts (Jobber & Lancaster,
2012).

Another possibility is the use of *team selling* which involves combined efforts of
sales reps, sales managers, and even engineers, and product specialists. When
building effective teams, questions to answer include: How can team members
benefit from each other when working together (i.e., joint customer meetings,
presentations, negotiations)? How can customers benefit from the team play on
the other hand? In addition, team selling provides a method of responding to
commercial, technical, and psychological requirements of large buying
organizations (Jobber & Lancaster, 2012).

Focusing on employee's strengths and utilizing those does not mean that managers
can ignore their weaknesses. That would be naive. Sales leaders should therefore
manage salespersons' potentials that are necessary to fulfill the job. Correct, we
deliberately said "manage" and not "try to minimize" the salesperson's weaknesses.
The reason is that someone will never be successful, where he has his weaknesses or
has eliminated those. This approach only brings a person to the level of mediocrity.

When managing the salesperson's potentials, the important question to ask is
whether the employee needs to change his behavior or his selling technique. Why?
In comparison, it is much more difficult to change a behavior pattern or attitude
toward sales rather than adopting particular selling techniques. When sales reps do
for instance cold calling to gain new customers, they may fight with negative
thoughts or inner blockades which hinders them to make calls as necessary. This
can happen for many reasons, including the pressure to achieve targets and negative
experiences with prospects (e.g., hearing a rigid "no" for the umpteenth time).

In accordance with Wimmer, Wimmer, Buchacher, and Kamp (2012), we
therefore suggest to do an *analysis of motivation* of the salesperson in question,
consisting of four questions: He or she. . .

- *Does not know*: Information, clarification, and support will help.
- *Is not able*: Support and training are the adequate reaction. Continuous learning
  control is in the following necessary. The ultima ratio is to offer the sales person
  another job or to go separate ways in future.
- *Is not allowed*: After analyzing the work process, the sales manager makes
  changes in the process. Note: Group standards and peer pressure ("This is how
  we always do it") can sometimes induce people not to act as they want. This
  demands working on group dynamics.

- *Does not want*: This is the most common assumption. If leaders believe this is the case, it is important to conduct a motivational performance review with the salesperson (see Sect. 6.4.5 for instructions). That includes questions about values in order to clarify the causes of motivation and demotivation. Narrow leadership as well as the threatening and implementation of consequences will be necessary.

Application questions for sales managers:

1. *Choose one of your low performers (hopefully, there is only one...).*
2. *Analyze briefly his motivation: He (a) does not know, (b) is not able, (c) is not allowed, or (d) does not want.*
3. *Following this, what are the next steps to do?*

---

4) Develop a Successful Team

The sales manager's task is not only to develop and deploy each sales rep according to his strengths and potentials but also to develop a successful team. The term "good teamwork" can become very easily an empty phrase. For that reason, Francis and Young (2012) developed a questionnaire, which looks at 12 team factors. Depending on how strong or weak each individual factor is, the criterion gives hints to possible difficulties in teamwork. The analysis helps sales managers to initiate targeted measures for the promotion of teamwork.

We therefore like to share Francis and Young's (2012) success factors for team development with you in the following:

1. *Effective team leadership*: The sales manager has the talent and willingness to work with his team closely and takes time for the development of it.
2. *Qualification*: The employees are qualified for their task and bring their skills to the team, so that a balanced mix of talent and personality arises.
3. *Commitment*: The team members identify themselves with the objectives and intentions of the team. They are willing to invest their energy in the development of the team and to assist other members.
4. *Positive climate*: Everyone feels good in the team. They can work with each other openly and directly.
5. *Team achievement*: The team knows its goals and decided that these are desirable. All members put their energy into achieving results.
6. *Relevant corporate role*: The team is involved in the overall plan and has a clearly defined and meaningful function within the sales organization.
7. *Effective meetings*: The team has found practical, systematic, and effective ways to commonly overcome problems.

8. *Role clarity*: Clearly defined roles, good flow of information, and administrative support are essential pillars of the team.
9. *Positive critiquing*: When talking about mistakes and weaknesses, team members do not personally attack each other in order to learn from the criticism.
10. *Personal development*: All team members are consciously looking for new experiences and bring their whole personality into service of the team.
11. *Team creativity*: The team has the ability to create ideas through teamwork, to promote innovative risks, and to benevolently accept and implement new ideas from inside or outside the group.
12. *Interteam relationships*: The team has built up relationships with other units to ensure open and optimal cooperation. The teams keep regular contact with each other and jointly agree on tasks and priorities. Interteam relationships are of particular importance, as we have discussed in Sect. 5.3. Smoothly functioning interfaces offer many benefits such as the creation of superior customer value by efficiently coordinating marketing activities.

6.2 Training and Development

Training is without doubt a central topic in nowadays sales. The question is where it is going to be linked to within the organization, so that it provides maximum results. Some may point out that it is a subdivision of leading a team. As we see the holistic approach, we strongly support the thought that training is a management topic. Because for the sales-driven organization—as discussed in Sect. 4.4—it has to be directly linked to top decision makers and be communicated and conducted "top-down."

Training, as will be seen in the following sections, affects the entire company. It does not only provide the technical support and the sales team with required knowledge and skills. Furthermore, it enables the complete staff how to transform top management decisions into persuasive activities. It starts with induction programs—which also includes "sales assistants" as a target group (to be discussed in the following section)—covers ongoing education, individual development, leadership, as well as team-building aspects. And it responds—if it is being done professionally—effectively to major incidents in daily business mainly coming from new legislation or competition. Therefore, it is in our view a vital part of sales management.

6.2.1 Importance and Benefits of Sales Trainings

Developing effective sales training programs has become an important part of a sales manager's job. Due to rapid changes in information technology, customers are now more knowledgeable than ever before. They get continuously more demanding in terms of quality and service. And they clearly develop ideas of what they are willing to pay and like to dictate what goes on.

This significant shift in the balance of power between the sales and the buying side has increasingly undermined the confidence of salespeople. Besides, the sales rep as lone wolf—as discussed in Chap. 5—gets progressively overwhelmed due to the increasing tasks he has to fulfill. This may become even worse, when there is not only one decision maker but a group of people. As a consequence, salespeople have to educate themselves and learn how to successfully cope with the current setup and new requirements in order to stay competitive.

With *sales training*, the sales force develops positive attitudes about their job ("inner mindset" as discussed in Sect. 5.2.2) and grows in knowledge, skills, and selling techniques. Sales training includes both

- *Formal programs* (i.e., structured courses or sessions that are aligned with learning and business goals)
- *Informal programs* (i.e., generally learner-driven and performed on an ad hoc basis, or as needed)

that are designed for *salespeople* to achieve the organization's overall, long-term goals.

The purpose of sales training should not only be limited to develop the sales team—the classical "front line of the company"—but all employees (including internal service, administrative, and technical staff). Turning them into, what we call, *"sales assistants"* ensures that customers receive the help they need fast, and with friendly, well-trained employees who are accessible for customers and fully aware of the importance of good customer relations.

Especially technical support staff is the company's most credible business card. Every customer prefers to ask a technician rather than a salesperson when considering a replacement or new investment. The only problem with technicians is their generally negative attitude toward sales. By convincing technical staff of the necessity of a more sales-oriented approach (1) by showing them what they can get out of it, (2) by systematically training them in conversational techniques, and (3) by intensifying the links to the salespeople with the resultant cross-fertilization of ideas, the customer-oriented approach can produce a very positive echo. And this will help to discover that price (fortunately!) is not everything.

If companies want to be successful in sales, they should attach utmost importance to train their staff. Both top managers and sales managers must be committed to training initiatives and authorize sufficient investment. Moreover, they should take into consideration that most benefits derived from sales training may not be immediate. They may take time to show through, but it is definitely worthwhile in the mid run.

The potential *benefits* of sales training are immense, ranging from higher company profits, increased productivity, improved moral, and greater self-confidence in one's ability to perform well at selling. A list of exemplary benefits is given in Table 6.3:

Table 6.3 Benefits of sales trainings

Enhanced skill development	Enhanced self-efficacy
Improved levels of performance	Increased sales volume
Reduced employee turnover	Improved customer relations
Increased organizational commitment	Decreased selling costs
Increased job satisfaction	Improved control of the sales force
Improved customer orientation	Improved used of time

Sources: Attia, Honeycutt, and Leach (2005), Krishnan, Netemeyer, and Boles (2002), Pettijohn, Pettijohn, and Taylor (2007)

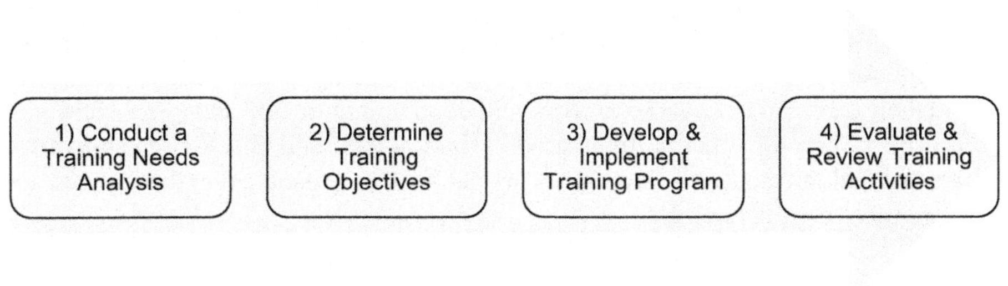

1) Conduct a Training Needs Analysis	2) Determine Training Objectives	3) Develop & Implement Training Program	4) Evaluate & Review Training Activities

Fig. 6.4 Sales training development process

6.2.2 Development of Sales Training Programs

Whether sales managers and trainers design initial or continuing sales training programs, they need to make several planning decisions. The sales training development process, shown in Fig. 6.4, lists the major decision areas

1) Conduct a Training Needs Analysis
The first step in developing a sales training program is to conduct a *training needs analysis* of the sales force. Sales managers should review the team to identify gaps between their current qualifications and the required job activities. The various profiles are discussed in Sect. 5.3.1. Sales managers can then develop customized sales training programs that are based on the developmental needs of each salesperson.

2) Determine Training Objectives
The specific objectives of sales training may vary from company to company. However, in terms of the broad objectives, there is some agreement. Sales training is usually undertaken for one or more of the following reasons:

- *Improve selling skills*: It attempts to teach and enhance critical skills in order to improve performance in the field. Through training, the sales force grows in know-how, capabilities, and selling techniques.

- *Improve moral*: It attempts to instill self-confidence and demonstrate the importance of the selling function to the company. Through training, the sales force develops positive attitudes about their job and motivation.
- *Lower employee turnover*: Sales training attempts to improve retention. If a salesperson quits, a customer who has been contacted by this person may transfer business to other suppliers. Fluctuation is costly. When a sales rep leaves, there is the cost of hiring and educating a new team member. Plus, there is a potential loss of profit during the transfer period.
- *Improve customer relations*: It attempts to adequately enable salespeople to fulfill their customers' needs, handling customer questions, objections, and complaints. The aim is to improve customer relations and promote their loyalty.
- *Improve teaming processes*: It attempts to develop good team players. Sales reps should not only deliver required results. They also stand behind their colleagues and their team, are enjoyable to work with, and communicate and keep everyone informed (among others). Interactive group works and discussions but also recreational breaks allow attendees to get to know each other better and to strengthen team behavior.

3) Develop and Implement Training Program
There are in general two types of sales training programs. *New intake training programs* (also known as "onboarding") are designed for newly hired salespeople. These comprehensive programs usually last from 4 weeks to 6 months. The goal is to teach new recruits the basic selling concepts, as well as knowledge about the company, products, competitors, markets, and customers.

Continuing sales training programs, on the other hand, are designed for experienced sales staff. These programs are usually much shorter and more intensive and cover specialized topics. When developing and implementing these programs, several decisions have to be made:

(A) *Determine content*: What is the training content?
(B) *Determine responsibility*: Who will train the sales force?
(C) *Choose training methods*: What methods will be used to transfer knowledge effectively?
(D) *Prepare attendees*: How will attendees be prepared for the training?
(E) *Motivate participants*: How will participants be motivated for learning?
    These questions will be answered in the following.

(A) Determine Content
Depending on the salesperson's knowledge and skill level, one or more of the following elements should be covered in the training program.

Selling Skills Training: Salespeople must learn the company's sales process (see Chap. 3). The main steps of this process are (1) prospecting and acquiring new customers, (2) building trust in the initial meeting, (3) identifying problems and needs, (4) making an individual offer and presenting convincing solutions based on the product's values, (5) conducting a confident price talk, (6) closing the deal, and (7) doing after-sales.

In each sales process step, attendees learn to apply the various selling techniques. For instance, in a training on "acquisition," trainees learn how to arrange appointments with prospects on the phone: How to formulate interesting "door openers"? How to handle and diminish objections (e.g., no time, no demand)? Besides "how-to" structures, sales training often includes a part about the essential inner attitude (e.g., handling a "no" from the prospect) since a negative view will hinder good sales performance as discussed in Sect. 5.2.2. These beliefs have to be broken up. As salespeople often have mainly one chance to meet with a prospect, most training time is devoted to presentation skills, such as presenting the benefits convincingly through verbal and nonverbal factors. Selling skills are often taught through role plays, as discussed later in the chapter.

Company Knowledge: Newly recruited salespersons should learn about the company's general policies, including the company benefits, payment methods, expense accounts, communication channels, and the office protocol (i.e., attitudes, etiquette rules, and guidelines for behavior that encompass the best way to act at work). They should also learn about specific selling policies and procedures: e.g., How many calls to make per day? How to handle customer requests (such as price adjustments, product modifications, faster delivery, and different credit terms)?

Product and Service Knowledge: The aim for product and service knowledge training is to better serve customers. As it is critical that the right product or service is applied to each customer's unique needs, salespeople should not only study what the product specifications exactly are and know how the product is used. They must also learn how to solve the customers' problems. Often customers want to know how the product meets their individual demand, and how competitive products compare on price, construction, performance, and compatibility with each other.

Market and Customer Knowledge: Salespeople need to know the market and their particular industry, including trends and competitive products and tactics. This is not only essential for forecasting sales and setting quotas but also for comparing brands, highlighting advantages of the own products, and overcoming customer objections. Salespeople must also have detailed knowledge about the customers. This includes information, among others, about the (1) contact person, (2) company, (3) products and services offered, (4) customer's customers, (5) problems and challenges faced, and (6) strategy and goals of the company.

Technology Training: Sales reps need to know how to use their technical equipment and software in order to plan their sales activities, write reports (e.g., about sales calls and customer meetings), check inventory and price levels, submit orders, and present product and service demonstrations. The aim of technology training is to improve the sales force productivity and help the organization accomplish its objectives efficiently.

(B) Determine Responsibility

Depending on the size of the company, different people are involved in the selection of the trainer. In large enterprises, the HR department is usually in charge of this process. In smaller companies, the managing director or the sales manager himself selects a trainer who then develops and delivers the training program. Responsibility for the execution of the training can belong to the sales manager, internal staff trainers, or external training specialists.

Sales Managers: Staff managers often train new as well as experienced salespersons. Out of their function, they are usually well respected, and their messages tend to carry authority in comparison to those of internal staff trainers and external training specialists. They are also in a better position to evaluate the salesperson's ability and performance than inside and outside staff trainers who have not seen the trainees performing in their daily business. If sales managers are not responsible for training, they should always participate in planning and developing the training program, as they are most familiar with strengths and needs of the sales force. We strongly recommend that sales managers should at least occasionally participate in every relevant training measure.

Internal Staff Trainers: Some companies establish and maintain a training department with staff trainers who are hired specifically for training purposes. Inside staff trainers have the time and teaching skills necessary for sales training. They develop training programs to teach salespeople how to sell the company's products and services effectively. The advantage is that they do have a deep understanding about products, internal structures, processes, and the company itself. The disadvantage is, however, that salespeople sometimes do not accept inside staff trainers completely as they only "theoretically train sales" but "do not operate in daily sales" anymore. Management support can help to overcome this problem.

External Training Specialists: Those specialists offer small to large companies flexibility because they can conduct an entire sales training program or handle a particular part a firm needs most. Since their market position depends on their client's satisfaction, external trainers usually have in general a profound sales background and practical knowledge—and therefore the street credibility—and good communication skills. A disadvantage is that they do lack in-depth market and product knowledge. When developing a training program, outside trainers should have a good understanding of the company's sales process, problems, and terminology and of the salespersons' attitude and skill level (i.e., individual needs, limitations, and prerequisites).

(C) Choose Training Methods

There are many methods of training available. Both traditional and recently emerged methods are used by all kind of trainers. The most typical ones are described below:

Classroom Training: Classroom courses, or face-to-face training, often include several methods. Through theoretical input, the trainer can present—or even better work out with participants—essential information on how to sell. Through single and group practical exercises, attendees can put theory into practice. For instance, if learning a structure on how to handle price objections, attendees can be asked to formulate typical examples in writing, which may then be discussed in feedback and fine-tuning sessions. The newly learned structures can also be practiced in role-playing activities as described below. Other methods are group discussions and experience exchanges to analyze and solve problems or to stimulate talk and participation by the attendees.

Role-Playing: Role-playing is learning by doing. Participants receive a daily business-related task. For example, they try to sell a product to a hypothetical customer or prospect—usually played by the trainer or another attendee. These activities can help participants learn to deal with critical people and unforeseen situations. If recorded by video, participants have the chance to see themselves and reflect on the situation. In this way, the trainer has the chance to work with participants on selling techniques (e.g., content and structures), verbal communication (e.g., voice and rhetoric), and body language (e.g., gestures and facial expressions).

Mentoring ("buddy systems"): Mentoring typically pairs a new or junior salesperson with an experienced colleague for a longer period of time—about 6 months to 2 years—with the goal of transferring knowledge and exchanging experiences. A list of advantages of mentoring programs is given in Table 6.4:

In Field Training: On-the-job training is an individual instructional method in which the trainee will be accompanied in the field by a more experienced salesperson. This may be the sales manager, a senior colleague, or a sales trainer. Typically, the trainee schedules 2–3 appointments with customers or prospects within 1 day. In between of the meetings, both evaluate the activities. The major advantage is that the trainee receives immediate feedback on his strengths and areas of improvement. He can directly work on improving his skills in the next appointment. However, for this method to be effective, the experienced salesperson must be qualified to train

Table 6.4 Advantages of mentoring programs

For the company	• Economic investment in the future • Low costs resulting from the internal staffing of future vacancies • Longer-term customer relationships by low sales staff turnover
For the sales manager	• Individual development perspective • Expansion of the personal qualifications • Use of mentors creates "open space" for sales management
For the new salesperson	• Fast "insider" information about company, customers, sales process • Increased productivity in customer contacts and faster success • Significant performance improvements through rapid feedback
For the experienced salesperson	• Focus on economic achievement • Focus on leadership • Cross-generation exchange

and influence the trainee. A major disadvantage is that it is costly and time-consuming for both people.

Electronic Training Methods: There are also Internet-based approaches available. In web conferencing, attendees use a computer screen to communicate with others via the Internet. With screen sharing, participants can see whatever is on the presenter's screen. They may then either respond via keyboard, through a traditional phone or speakerphone, or by Voice-over-Internet Protocol (VoIP). A webinar, a variation of web conferencing, is designed to be more interactive between presenter and audience. The software used for that includes both speaking and visual capabilities. Usually, webinars can be used for educational settings—especially when giving and receiving information, asking questions, exchanging opinions, and problem-solving. Webinars also work in conjunction with face-to-face training.

Note: Webinars will become more important in the future. The advantages are resources driven: better time efficiency and easy to attend and conduct. Nevertheless, they lack quality-wise: less individual and missing the elementary "human touch" in terms of practical exercises, personal feedback, and emotional chemistry.

(D) Prepare Attendees

When attendees do not understand why they are being trained and how they benefit from it, the effectiveness of every activity will be much lower. To increase the positive results of sales training, managers should prepare their sales force ahead of time. This can be done in one or more ways:

Preview of the Contents: The sales manager and trainer may want to forward the agenda of the workshop to all attendees. This approach has three key advantages. First, it helps salespeople to demystify the plain message "We will do training on initial talk!" They clearly know then what will occur in the workshop. Second, as discussions, experience exchanges, practical exercises, and role-playing activities are seen as "close to business reality," the agenda helps people to understand the seriousness and helpfulness of a training initiative. Sales training is not just "blah blah," but a high standard, well-structured, and practical-oriented method to improve participants' ability to sell. Third and finally, the agenda helps attendees to warm up much quicker and to arrive already generally prepared at the start of the training session. An example is shown in Fig. 6.5.

Pre-course Worksheets: In order to have participants arrive ready to learn, the sales superior and trainer may also want to give participants a pre-course worksheet. This exercise, for instance, can ask attendees to prepare practical exercises and answer training-related questions which lay the foundation of single and group works and role-playing activities. As all participants are specifically prepared, this tool provides a much quicker and steeper learning curve. An example for preparing a role play is given in Fig. 6.6.

Kick-Off: If it is a particularly important sales topic, the sales manager—or a member of senior management—can personally kick-off the training. This is a valid tool not only to enhance its credibility but also to confirm corporate support and to illustrate the "management attention." To achieve this, the sales manager should

---

AGENDA (Excerpt)

Sales Workshop: Successful Initial Talk & Needs Assessment

Wednesday, 25th of January (Start: 9:00 am):

- Welcome speech by Sales Manager: My expectations for this workshop = Practical tools
- Defining a Key-Account profile according to the current market situation
- Exercise: Making a convincing first impression (with video)
- My own appearance – vital elements and effect mechanisms of body language
- Video-analysis with individual feedback by trainer and colleagues
- …

Fig. 6.5 Example of agenda (Excerpt)

PRE-COURSE WORKSHEET (Excerpt)

Practical Exercise: Initial Meeting

Your perception:

On a scale of 1 to 10, with 10 being the highest, how would a prospect rate the way you create a convincing "first impression" (e.g. Think about your last meeting with a prospect):

          1   2   3ʹ   4   5   6   7   8   9   10

Supporting statement (to illustrate your score): _____

Your task:

On the first day of the training, you will be asked to do a role play with two or three of your colleagues in front of a video camera (approx. 2-3 minutes). This is your exercise:

You will now meet a new contact person <u>for the first time</u>. Please create a convincing first impression to secure a successful strategic cooperation.

Please choose a realistic scenario in advance:

What is the name of the company? _____
What is the type of the organization (sector, size, location)? _____
Who is attending the meeting (names and functions)? _____

In the training, you will have another 5 minutes to prepare your role play. Later on, you will receive an individual feedback on your strengths and potentials.

Fig. 6.6 Example of pre-course worksheet (Excerpt)

explain purpose and objectives of the training, benefits for the attendees, and his specific expectations toward the workshop. This information also helps the trainer in the following to align with the announcement and to get important messages across.

(E) Motivate Participants:
If attendees are not motivated to participate during the training, learning does not sufficiently occur ("emotional buy-in"). There are several ways how sales managers and trainers get salespeople motivated for learning. Spitzer (1995) suggests the following strategies, among others, to motivate trainees:

- *Just-in-time training*: Attendees are motivated to learn, when they perceive a real need for training. The sales manager can ensure this by explaining why attendees have an urgent need for these new skills (e.g., business performance of the company).
- *Active training formats and variety*: The trainer should limit the amount of theoretical input and build involvement into the session by including written activities, discussions, demonstrations, games, and role-playing activities.
- *Social interaction*: Social interaction can motivate attendees. The trainer should encourage this by including simulations, small-group discussions, and collaborative problem-solving exercises.
- *Safe environment*: So that attendees are eager to learn and use new skills, fear must be minimized. This can be achieved by announcing that everything said is confidential and that there are no mistakes, only learning opportunities.
- *Sufficient practice*: The amount of practice required to gain proficiency often tends to be underestimated. The trainer should encourage attendees to practice their new skills on the job by scheduling follow-up activities.

4) Evaluate and Review Training Activities
Once a training program has been carried out, it is essential to evaluate its effectiveness and how well the training objectives and goals have been met. Kirkpatrick (1979) proposes a four-stage training model for evaluating training programs:

1. *Reaction*: Reactions are measures about the attendees' attitudes, feelings, and satisfaction with the training program to determine how well it was accepted. For instance, attendees can be interviewed, or they can complete forms, surveys, and comment sheets.
2. *Learning*: Having a competent and inspiring trainer does not necessarily lead to learning. The change in attitude and the acquisition and retention of knowledge can be assessed by pen and paper tests before and after the training and/or by training activities such as demonstrations, role-playing situations, and the individual performance of the skill being taught.
3. *Behavior*: Behavior change evaluations measure the extent to which salespersons modify their job-related behavior as a result of sales training activities. The sales manager can observe attendees in the workplace and/or accompany them in the field.
4. *Results*: Both individual and company-wide performance evaluations measure the extent to which a sales training has contributed to the achievement of its training objectives. Managers, for instance, measure change in profit and sales, selling costs, customer relations, and staff turnover.

Table 6.5 Planning of sales training programs

Performance needs analysis	Training needs analysis	Feasibility analysis
• What is the key problem? • What should happen instead? • What factors help and hinder employee performance? • What precise improvements do you expect from the trainees? • What improvements do you hope for in your organization?	• What will be taught? • What needs to be included? • How will it be presented? • Who will present it? • What do employees already know about the topic? • What should they be able to do afterward?	• Is the training solution really practical? • Does the training have management support? • Is the budget available? • What are the technical/organizational requirements?

Source: Adapted from Chase (1997, p. 28)

6.2.3 Typical Sales Training Mistakes

There are common training mistakes which mislead investments and result in not reaching targets. Some of those mistakes are a waste of time and money—not only for the company but also for each attendee who could have done selling in the meantime. Possible solutions to avoid these classical traps are summarized below.

1) *Lack of preparation*: The greatest mistake that sales managers make in developing sales training programs is a lack of planning. However, preparation is the Alpha and Omega. This includes a thorough analysis of the company's needs and objectives, a comprehensive analysis of training needs, and a financially and operationally feasible design of training interventions. Important questions to ask are listed in Table 6.5 (Chase, 1997):

2) *Lack of communication to participants in advance*: All too often, participants do not see the intended reason of the training. But just like customers and prospects, they want to know "what's in it for me?" Participants also like to know what are the causes for conducting the training. This question should be answered by management when announcing the training or—at the very latest—when the training starts so that everyone is aligned.

3) *Lack of involvement of participants*: Sales training is about enabling people. Just giving theoretical input is not enough to achieve a difference in attitude, behavior, and performance. Instead, training should be established in a way that attendees are able to practically work through the topics. Involvement can be built, for example, by including brainstorming, discussions, role plays, and written activities.

4) *Uninteresting content and boring approach*: Nearly everyone has been through at least one training that was rather dry in terms of content and delivery. For a positive experience and worthwhile investment, the trainer should have energy, commitment, and fun delivering the session so that the spark jumps over. In addition, the trainer should rather be over-prepared so that he can flexibly react

to unforeseen situations. Moreover, the content should be customized to the audience. The easier attendees can understand the correlation to what they do in their daily business, the more likely they buy into it. Also, practical examples from the field—such as success and failure stories—will grab and maintain the audience's interest.

5) *Lack of positive feedback*: Why is it difficult to find a first volunteer in doing a role play? Participants may fear not knowing the answer, thus appearing to be a fool, or they may be frightened that the trainer is picking on them by telling them how bad they did. As a result, attendees are often reluctant of sharing their ideas and actively doing practical exercises. In fact, every person is good in something and this should be recognized by giving positive feedback. Our rule of thumb: One negative point of criticism should be followed by two positive remarks. Moreover, voluntary participation should be encouraged and recognized—especially in sales trainings since selling is about proactively influencing others.

6) *Lack of goal setting for daily business and follow-up*: Many sales trainings are ineffective because they abruptly finish with the end of the training session. What then follows is that the content is forgotten quickly, and the same old behaviors and habits continue. Therefore, it is important that a clear objective of what the training should accomplish is set. Following this, at the end of the training, each participant should establish a personal target agreement of what and how he concretely wants to achieve within the next weeks in his daily business (with hard facts and figures). The sales manager should then arrange follow-ups to the training and communicate to all participants what is expected of them, and how they will be measured and rewarded.

6.3   Recruitment and Induction of the Right Talents

The best strategies are useless, if there is nobody to professionally put them into practice and live them out on the "front line." What salespeople say and how they interact with prospects and customers influences the firm's success decisively. The trouble is that good salespeople are a "rare species" and very difficult to find. Furthermore, every industry watches out for those special ones. Like in football, every club is almost constantly looking for talented strikers.

Even a seemingly good candidate with a great curriculum vitae (CV) and convincing qualifications may not necessarily prove an ideal fit for the company. Hiring the wrong salesperson costs companies ten-thousands in salary, benefits, training, and lost productivity. That is why nearly all sales organizations are searching desperately for the right *sales talents*:

- Who easily integrate themselves into the company culture
- Who are self-motivated in their everyday work
- Who are resilient in facing difficulties

- Who rapidly understand all products and types of customers
- Who quickly perform up to their 100% target
- Who constantly perform well
- Who are likely to stay for the long run

As the "war for sales talents" will only intensify in future, observing the market (scouting) should be an ongoing activity at least for all larger companies. *Recruitment* and *selection* is in these competitive times for every enterprise a vital element in achieving their goals. Unfortunately, many organizations wait until they have a vacancy to begin the recruitment process. One drawback of this approach is that due to the short-term acting, it limits the pool of suitable candidates that are available. A second drawback is that sales managers can fall prey to nervousness and hire too quickly someone new—but not "right." Finally, sales units may also lose sales opportunities to the competition when no one is covering the territory in the meantime.

Organizations should also establish effective *induction* programs for newly hired sales staff. Due to the fact that it is likely that talented people are being contacted or scouted by competitive firms, it is important to give them convincing reasons to join. Professional onboarding programs are a persuasive argument for hiring high potentials. Besides, every (sales) job takes some time to learn. To achieve the ambitious objective of 100% revenue within a short period of time (e.g., probation period), it is therefore required to run a high-quality educational program. So that sales reps are quickly enabled and brought up to speed for their competitive profession.

6.3.1   The Recruitment and Selection Process

To ensure that newly hired people have the aptitude necessary to be successful in a particular sales position, it is best to follow a systematic step-by-step process through which recruitment and selection is carried out. The process is shown in Fig. 6.7:

In the beginning, it is necessary to decide who will have the primary *responsibility for recruitment and selection*. The way in which this question is being answered typically depends on the size of the company and the sales force and the complexity of its products and services. In enterprises with smaller sales forces, the sales manager often is responsible for hiring new sales reps. In larger sales units, the job of attracting and choosing sales candidates is too time-consuming and expensive for a single person. In such firms, internal recruiting specialists (normally as part of the HR department)—or outside consultants—help in attracting sales applicant. They also assist in screening and evaluating candidates and advice sales managers in hiring the right people. The sales manager, however, typically has the final call.

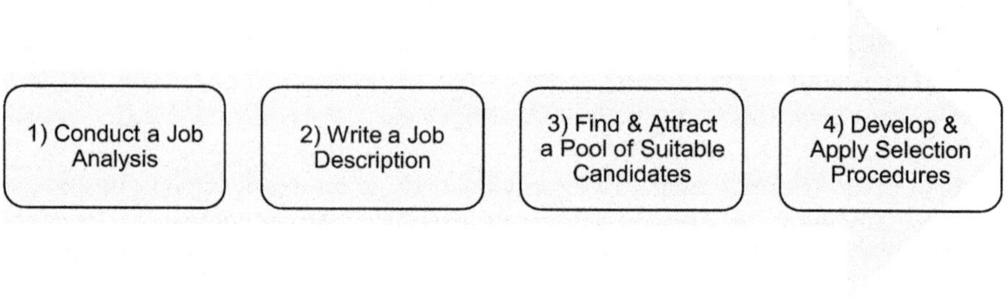

| 1) Conduct a Job Analysis | 2) Write a Job Description | 3) Find & Attract a Pool of Suitable Candidates | 4) Develop & Apply Selection Procedures |

Fig. 6.7 Recruitment and selection process

1) Conduct a Job Analysis

The first step in this process is to conduct a profound job analysis. This determines which activities, responsibilities, and environmental influences are involved in this position (Johnston & Marshall, 2013). A proper job analysis typically covers the following dimensions:

(A) Job qualifications and conditions:
   • What knowledge, skills, and professional and educational background are needed for the position?
   • What personal and social skills are required?
   • What is the amount of travel involved?
(B) Activities and responsibilities:
   • What core tasks must be fulfilled by the job holder?
   • What specific responsibility is transferred to the sales person?
   • What developmental opportunities exist or can arise?
(C) Relationship between job holder, superior, and other positions within the company:
   • To whom does the salesperson report, and on what occasion?
   • What are the salesperson's specific duties to the immediate supervisor?
   • How and when does the salesperson interact with other departments of the company?
(D) Environmental influences:
   • What is the nature of products or services to be sold?
   • What kinds of customers will be handled by the employee?
   • What environmental factors and constraints might influence job performance?

The required information can be generally collected from two sources: (1) current salespeople can be observed or interviewed, or both, in order to determine what they actually do. This can be done for different types of customers and over a representative period of time; (2) the superior can be asked what the job holder should be doing, especially in view of the company's strategic objectives, and what is expected to be highly relevant in the near future (e.g., market trends).

Job Description

1) Job title:

2) Main tasks:

3) Candidate profile:
  - Education (*e.g. technical background, business background, apprenticeship, study*):
  - Experience:
  - Knowledge & skills (*e.g. technical, methodological, and social competence*):

4) Special features (*e.g. travel activity*):

5) Reporting structure:

6) Terms & conditions of the employment contract:
  (*e.g. salary range, vacation days, employment probation*)

Fig. 6.8 Job description

2) Write a Job Description

The result of a formal analysis is a precise job description which explains—to applicants and current position holders—the tasks and responsibilities of the position, knowledge, experience, and skills needed on the job. This gives for the following steps in the recruitment process, especially for the interviews, a good orientation. Sales candidates then know exactly what is expected of them before they accept their job (Hair et al., 2010).

The job description will not only be used for recruitment and selection efforts but also as guide for conducting regular performance reviews, fixing salaries, deciding about promotions, and designing training programs. Therefore, the job description must naturally be in writing so that everyone can refer to it when necessary. An example is shown in Fig. 6.8. It is important to review it constantly to ensure that it accurately presents the current scope and activities of the particular sales position.

3) Find and Attract a Pool of Suitable Candidates

There are basically two types of channels for finding suitable candidates. As shown in Fig. 6.9, *internal channels* consist of people who work already for the company, whereas *external channels* include people from other companies, educational institutions, and recruitment agencies. In order to cope successfully with the existing war for talents, firms should utilize as many sources as possible—sequentially or in parallel. It is useful that companies analyze the potential sources to determine which produces the best recruits for the sales position to be filled. These are outlined in the following (Hair et al., 2010):

Within the Company: Enterprises can promote current employees from non-sales departments. The advantage is that these people are familiar with the company's products, policies, and operations. They have an established performance record. Thus, firms know the candidates' strengths and areas of improvement. In addition, internal recruiting may bolster company morale, as other employees become aware of developmental opportunities. However, people from other departments seldom

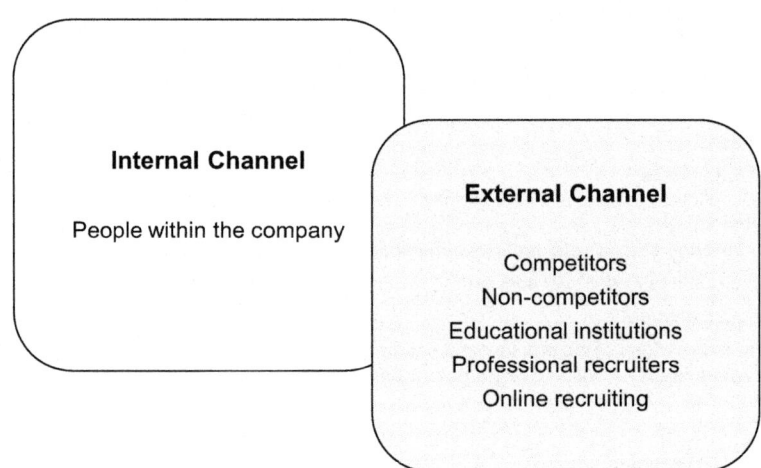

Fig. 6.9 Sources for finding suitable candidates

have much previous selling experience. Out of this, they usually require additional skill and knowledge training.

Competitors: The question of whether a company should recruit salespersons from competing firms is controversial. The advantage is that these people should be ready to sell almost immediately, since they are trained and experienced in selling familiar products and services to similar markets. Moreover, they bring "new vibes" and different approaches to the company and positively disturb the existing balance in the sales team. However, the practice of recruiting direct competitor's salespeople is sometimes viewed as unethical. These issues especially arise when such people are expected to bring along and serve some of their current customers or divulge valuable proprietary information from the former company. Hiring a salesperson from a competing firm may also pose some legal questions, if they have signed a noncompetition agreement with their former employer.

Noncompetitors: Closely related companies can provide a good source of candidates, especially if they sell relatively similar products and services or serve the same markets. Also companies that are either vendors or customers of the recruiting firm can be a good source of trained and experienced sales staff. In most cases, these recruits also have some knowledge about the company and are familiar with the industry which, in turn, reduces the time it takes to make them productive.

Educational Institutions: Enterprises can also recruit candidates directly from high schools, adult evening classes, and universities. This is especially promising from those educational institutions which have specialized sales programs in place. While most graduates lack specific sales experience, these recruits have the educational background and perspective required. Due to their young age, they also tend to adapt more easily and have not established "dogmatic habits" yet. They have also in general not developed preferences for a particular company or industry.

Professional Recruiters: Companies can select professional recruiters that are specialized in hiring sales employees. They usually provide a full range of services, from searching for candidates to screening, interviewing, and recommending the best sales candidates. The quality of results often depends on the working relationship between the recruiter and the sales manager. Especially by establishing a reliable relationship, and by providing detailed information about the vacant position, the agency can perform a valuable service. If internal HR resources are limited, an important advantage of external recruiters is the reduction of time and effort that sales managers must devote to recruiting. Additionally, they provide a broad database of potential candidates which can be quickly addressed.

One additional remark: The search for highly skilled sales talents—with particular industry expertise—often corresponds to the search for the needle in a haystack. In this case, companies more and more use a specialized recruitment service: *direct search*. Those recruitment professionals research the availability of suitable candidates, which work for competitors or related businesses. They identify a shortlist of qualified candidates, who match their client's requirements. In most cases, direct search professionals contact potential candidates themselves and see if they might be interested in moving to a new employer. Direct search firms may also accompany the entire recruitment process (up to signing the work contract) and may give advice, e.g., in terms of salary negotiations.

Online Recruiting: Companies increasingly use professional network platforms such as LinkedIn and Xing to contact potential sales candidates. These platforms also offer particular electronic recruiting solutions to companies. Many enterprises additionally use career services such as Monster and StepStone which are databases that post job listings from companies. Recruiting online has some advantages. It allows access to more people and a broader selection of applicants, and it enables companies to target the type of people needed. However, some corporations are concerned about the high volume of résumés and their limited resources to view them.

4) Develop and Apply Selection Procedures

After some sales candidates have applied for the job, the next task is to determine which applicants best meet the qualifications, have the greatest aptitude for the job, and best fit the company culture (see Schneider, 1987 for person-organization fit). Except for initial screening, Homburg, Schäfer, and Schneider (2002) suggest that one or more of the following tools and procedures can aid the selection process. Sometimes they are also combined in assessment centers (AC), especially for management positions. Let's discuss these in more detail:

Initial Screening: The purpose of it is to eliminate unsuitable applicants as soon as possible. Sales managers and recruiters can use various forms, such as (1) screening the résumé, (2) conducting a first phone or online video interview, and (3) asking to do some type of brief online test. The goal is to find in short time the right candidates for the next round (Hair et al., 2010). Note: The better the job description, the shorter the process.

Application Blanks: Although job applicants often have to submit résumés to prospective employers, larger companies frequently use an additional company application form. Through this kind of standardization, it is easier to assess and to compare candidates. These forms—mainly filled out online—in many cases collect information about the candidate's basic information, education, business experience, and personal interests. The information obtained is not only used to screen for basic qualifications but also to help managers and recruiters prepare for personal interviews with the sales candidates. The input can also be used to build up a database and establish a pool of candidates for future vacancies.

Reference Checking: This is a screening tool that enables sales managers and recruiters to obtain information from former bosses, clients, and other professionals to check the credibility of a job applicant. To make this happen, candidates are asked to provide references on the application form or later on in the process. In general, however, the quality of these reference checks is questionable as applicants would not give names of people who will speak badly of him.

Personal Interviews: This method is in our view the most effective tool to screen suitable sales candidates. Interviews enable sales managers and recruiters to get to know the candidate personally. A face-to-face interview is strongly recommended. It provides with the possibility to assess the candidate's communication skills, sociability, cognitive skills, empathy, ambition, and other traits that are necessary to be successful in the particular position. In fact, as many as 2–3 rounds of interviews should be usually conducted with the most desirable candidates. Sales managers and recruiters can use three different methods of conducting personal interviews.

- *Structured interviews*: Each candidate is asked the same set of standardized questions. The advantage is that it makes it easier to compare the individual strengths and weaknesses. One potential drawback is, however, that the interviewer may fail to identify the unique qualities of each applicant.
- *Unstructured interviews*: Such informal and nondirected interviews seek to get the candidates to talk freely on a variety of subjects. The interviewer only asks a few questions to direct the conversation to topics of interest. The advantage of this approach is to get a deeper insight into the applicant's personality, attitudes, and opinions. Difficulties are the comparability of answers of two or more candidates, as well as the influence of sympathy and antipathy.
- *Semi-structured interviews*: Many companies use a combination of structured and unstructured approaches. The interviewer asks a fixed set of questions and allows time for interaction and discussion. This is a very flexible approach and can be tailored to the needs of candidates and interviewers.

All three forms require a skilled interviewer. What is essential here is good empathy, strong questioning techniques, profound listening skills—especially "between the lines"—and deep sales know-how. We recommend that interviews are being conducted as a team of two people: One person conducts the conversation,

---

Interview Guide for Sales Positions (Excerpt)

First phase: The candidate will be asked to present himself
e.g.: "Walk me through your career progression leading up to your current role."
Interesting aspects are noted by the interviewer, and will be asked later on.
Interposed questions depend on the "standing" of the candidate.

Second phase: The candidate will be asked specific role-related questions
The questions below illustrate the possibilities of a targeted use of questioning techniques during an interview.

Exemplary questions for candidates in a sales position
"What sales goals have you had last year?", "What was your target achievement?"
"Do you have a "race list" in your company? What position do you have and why?"
"What do you love about field work and what you would like to give up?"

Further questions can be posed about (examples only)
Company: "What do you know about our company?"
Education: "If you could now do something else, what would it be?"
Career: "Please describe a typical day in your current position."
Work attitude: How would you describe your work style?
Personality: "What motivates you to do your best on the job?"
Other questions: "What are your salary expectations?"

Third phase: The candidate will be asked to do a practical exercise (optional)
Sales candidates must be able to do a "spontaneous sales pitch".
Task: The candidate is asked to explain why you want to purchase the firm's product.

Fourth phase: The candidate will be informed about the company and job function
After the candidate has given a comprehensive impression of his person, he receives information about the company, products & services, market development, job position, hierarchical levels and classification of the position in question, contract.

Fifth phase: End of interview
The interviewer checks if all questions and issues have been clarified.
The candidate will be informed about the next steps in the selection process, and when to expect feedback from the interviewer.

Fig. 6.10 Interview guide for sales positions (Excerpt)

while the other observes mainly. An interview guide for sales positions, as derived from our experience, is shown in Fig. 6.10.

Role-Play Exercises: Candidates for sales positions must be able to do a "spontaneous sales pitch." Companies, for instance, can ask applicants to explain to a potential customer "Why should I buy product x?" Of course, in this moment, the technical content is secondary. More interestingly, the interviewer gets an idea about two things: (1) how does the candidate deal with an unfamiliar situation and (2) how good does the applicant deliver the presentation. Interviewers can also ask aspirants to present themselves: "Why are you the ideal candidate?"

Formal Testing: Written tests are an objectified way to measure mental abilities and personality traits of candidates for sales positions and to increase the chances of selecting the right salespeople. The most commonly used tests are (Hair et al., 2010):

- *Intelligence tests* are helpful for assessing whether a candidate has sufficient mental abilities to perform the job successfully. These tests measure, for instance, logical reasoning, memory, and verbal ability.
- *Sales aptitude tests* evaluate an applicant's innate and acquired social skills and selling know-how.
- *Personality tests* measure behavioral traits—such as assertiveness, initiative, and empathy—that the test designer believes are necessary for being successful in a particular sales position.

Pre-employment testing is one of the most controversial tools in the selection process. Critics not only question the methodology used to develop these tests. Some sales managers also doubt that tests are valid for predicting the future success of salespeople. A related concern is that some talented people may be rejected simply because their personalities do not conform to test norms. Another issue involves the possible reactions of the applicants who are tested. They may select answers that they think the sales manager or recruiter wants to hear. As a result, tests should never be the sole criterion used in making hiring decisions.

6.3.2   Induction of New Salespeople

Hiring a sales person starts with the recruitment and selection process and ends with the induction process of the new colleague to the company. The aim of induction programs is to help salespeople to adjust as easily and effectively as possible to their new role, working environment, and particularly the company culture. These programs can also play a critical role in the socialization process. Benefits include greater job satisfaction, job involvement, and employee commitment (Dubinsky, Howell, Ingram, & Bellenger, 1986). It offers close contact with experienced sales staff and provides social support from other members of the company. In order to fully benefit the organization and salesperson, induction programs need to be planned in advance and should—to a certain degree—be standardized. For big enterprises, it is useful to conduct those programs on a regular basis (e.g., starting first week every quarter).

Compilation of Onboarding Plans

After the candidate has accepted his job offer, the HR department or the sales manager create an onboarding plan for a specific period of time. The aim is not only to eliminate inefficiencies and miscommunications but also to bring the new employee up to speed quickly. The length and content of induction programs will vary depending on the nature of the new salesperson's role. They usually take place over a number of weeks or months. (It is certainly not a 1-day event.) The onboarding plan lists all induction topics, time frames, and staff members who

Table 6.6 Onboarding plan: Week 1 (Excerpt)

Responsibility	Topic	Date	Time
DAY 1			
Sales manager	Welcome	01/05	2 h
	General overview		
HR department	Introduction	01/05	1 h
	Organizational matters		1 h
	Lunch		1 h
	About company and job		3 h
DAY 2			
Product management	Overview of product range	02/05	2 h
	Product X		
	• Workshop on X		3 h
	• Break		1 h
	• Presentation on X		2 h
DAY 3			
Product management	Market analysis	03/05	2 h
Production	Basics of production	03/05	2 h
	Product assembly		4 h
DAY 4			
Back office sales	General understanding of procedures, and processes	04/05	8 h
	Responsibilities		
	Q&A's		
DAY 5			
Sales rep	Participation in daily business	05/05	7 h
New sales rep	Wrap-up of first week	05/05	1 h

will be responsible for each activity. The plan will be circulated to everyone involved in the induction process, including the new colleague (see Bradt & Vonnegut, 2009 for in-depth knowledge on onboarding). An example of an onboarding plan is given in Table 6.6.

Introductory Trainings

Most companies prepare *detailed presentations and manuals* to inform new sales recruits about the company's history, product line, organization, and benefit packages. New salespeople—especially those who will work in the field—should be introduced to office and field operations of the company. This includes as well information about travel expenses, procedures, and policies.

Freshly hired sales recruits should participate in *new intake training programs*, which normally last from weeks to months. The aim is to teach them the basic selling concepts, as well as knowledge about the company, products, competitors, markets, and customers. In most cases, classroom training and field accompaniments with senior sales representatives take place before they act on their own responsibility. How to train sales people is discussed in detail in Sect. 6.2.

Salespeople are the company's main link to customers and prospects. Hence, new recruits should quickly understand the *inter-departmental interfaces and processes* between sales and the traditionally "sales-averse" departments such as production, administration, and R&D (as discussed in Sect. 4.2). By rotating 1–5 days in each of these departments—of course depending on the specific sales function—the new sales rep is able to experience the big picture, and:

- Deepens his knowledge about products and services on offer
- Comes to know colleagues who could have an impact on his role and his daily business, and most importantly,
- Can better consult and proactively influence customers and prospects

Mentoring programs ("Buddy systems")
New salespeople should get a mentor by their side. In our experience, this is rarely done and out of the ordinary. Having a mentor—or so-called "buddy"—makes a huge difference to the speed and quality at which new recruits manage to settle into their job role, department, and company. In most cases, it is a more experienced colleague who will be responsible for some or all of the following:

- Helping the new recruit to navigate his way around the department and company
- Showing the new colleagues how to do aspects of their role, for instance, by doing field accompaniments (e.g., making phone calls and visiting customers together)
- Introducing them to other colleagues who are important to their role (e.g., from product management, back office, IT)
- Helping new recruits to understand the formal and informal culture and structures, as well as internal procedures
- Encouraging new recruits to pose critical questions
- Socializing (e.g., arranging to go for lunch so new recruits feel part of the team)
- Using devices according to company standards (e.g., software, laptop)

6.4   Evaluating Salespeople

Performance Appraisals
Sales is—like professional sports—very result oriented. A pretty common question from C-level executives and senior management is: "Are we on track?" The purpose of regular performance appraisals is therefore to provide sales leaders with a framework to manage their sales force. These tools help:

- To recognize high-performing salespeople (e.g., with increased compensation or promotion), and to deny these benefits to low-performing salespeople or, if necessary, to dismiss them
- To identify training needs of salespeople

- To motivate and guide employees, and to give constructive feedback "from outside"
- To augment salespeople's future performance
- To establish an individual performance track record over time
- To identify high potentials for future leading positions
- To develop a compensation plan designed to encourage salespeople to sell certain products and services (e.g., by means of higher commission rates)

Due to the nature of the selling job, there are several challenges in evaluating salespeople. First, they usually work in the field and may have relatively little direct contact with their sales manager. Second, they have more information about their territory than their superior. They may use this information leadership to their advantage or may resort to excuses, such as "I do not have time for this!" or "I tried this already." Third, sales reps are engaged in many activities. It may be difficult to determine which tasks to evaluate—not forgetting their relative significance. Fourth, salespeople cannot control all factors that contribute to their individual performance. These can, for instance, include differences in territory potentials, intensity of competition, and salesperson tenure in the territory.

Finally, sad but true, sales managers quite often do a poor job in evaluating their sales force. In most cases because they dislike this particular task and feel uncomfortable having to assess the performance of their subordinates. Those, in return, often dislike being evaluated, especially if the final result is likely to be negative. From our observation, this task is pretty often postponed due to—as often heard— "heavy workload and different priorities."

6.4.1 The Salesperson Evaluation Process

Sales force performance evaluation is the comparison of given goals with achieved results. The systematic process for successful salesperson performance evaluations is shown in Fig. 6.11.

1) Establish Sales Targets

After top management has announced the company's goals and objectives for the upcoming period, the salesperson performance evaluation process can begin. The sales manager's first task is to derive specific objectives and goals for his sales force. This step includes the determination of both long-run goals such as being recognized by customers as the most service-oriented sales organization in the industry and short-term goals. The latter are more quantifiable objectives, called sales targets. Annual objectives could include increasing sales volume by x percent and keeping selling expenses within assigned budgets.

Sales targets can be assigned to particular sales units, including the sales organization, regions, districts, territories, (new/active) accounts, and individual salespersons. After having set the objectives and goals for his team, the sales

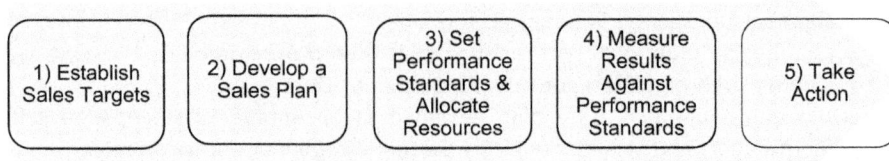

Fig. 6.11 Salesperson evaluation process

manager must ensure that every team member understands, accepts, and supports them (e.g., via written approval sheet).

2) Develop a Sales Plan
Next, a written sales plan must be developed which provides a detailed "road map" of how to achieve the—usually pretty ambitious—sales targets. This is normally being done through the same top-down approach as discussed in step 1. The development of the sales plan—typically being called forecast—should include five questions that need to be answered:

1. Where are we now? (i.e., market situation, competition, market share, sales, and customer situation)
2. Where do we need to go? (i.e., opportunities and problems in the internal and external environment)
3. How do we get there? (i.e., strategies and tactics, target customers, rollout)
4. Until when do we get there? (i.e., milestones and timeline)
5. Who is responsible for which activities? (i.e., individual tasks)

3) Set Performance Standards and Allocate Resources
The third step is to set performance standards that are expected to be achieved by the sales force throughout the year. They represent a mutual agreement between sales manager and salesperson, as to what level of performance is expected in the coming period. This usually happens in goal setting conversations, in which they jointly agree on specific performance targets.

The most important performance measures (to be discussed later)—known as key performance indicators (KPIs)—are then used to assess the salesperson's effectiveness. In this regard, sales managers should not only use quantitative measures (e.g., percentage of sales quota achieved) but also qualitative measures (e.g., report preparation and submission), because sales figures do not provide a complete assessment of the salesperson's job. This is particularly true in B2B sales, where it is likely to take several months or even years' lead time, before the prospect makes a final decision on buying.

After developing a set of goals, including standards of performance, both the sales manager and sales rep should establish the means of reaching these targets through, e.g., formal education, training, field accompaniments, or self-study activities. Finally, the sales manager must allocate resources (i.e., personnel and tangible assets) to achieve the desired goals.

4) Measure Results Against Performance Standards

Sales managers should continuously monitor and analyze individual performance relative to their assigned sales quotas and less quantifiable sales-related activities. As discussed by Hair et al. (2010), MBOprogram (to be discussed later) can be invaluable at this stage. It includes (1) *performance appraisals* that are conducted on a continuous basis, whereby sales managers give individual sales representatives immediate feedback. This can be recognition, correction, and or criticism on specific tasks, projects, or sales targets. Furthermore, an MBO program includes (2) a *performance review* that is conducted with each salesperson at the end of the period. It is a sum up of all performance appraisals so that the salesperson can see where he stands and where to go from there. Note: The more regular the meetings are being conducted, the more likely it is that results are on track.

5) Take Action

After making a detailed evaluation, the sales manager must take action based on the performance appraisal and performance review. Managers may need (1) to adjust the goals and objectives for sales force, (2) to revise the sales plan in terms of strategies and tactics used, and/or (3) to correct action of the salesperson's effort by enhancing the individual's personal development or modifying the company's procedures or methods of operation.

Before the sales manager presents an evaluation, the salesperson could be asked to make a self-evaluation and suggest precise ways to improve (e.g., defining clear activities). They can then compare both approaches, discuss discrepancies in evaluation perceptions, uncover causes of performance gaps, and take corrective action (e.g., exploiting the salesperson's strengths and reducing any weaknesses). A guide on how to conduct motivational performance reviews and giving constructive criticism is outlined in Sect. 6.4.5.

6.4.2   Performance Measures

Performance evaluations include both objective (quantitative) and subjective measures (qualitative). These two aspects are assigned different weights. Sales manager should generally provide feedback in both written and oral form and typically put greater emphasis on objective measures, as it leaves less room for controversial discussions. Anyhow, out of our experience, written feedback is a classical shortage and should be used far more often.

Table 6.7 Quantitative measures of sales performance

Orders	Profit
Average order value	Gross or net profit
Number of orders obtained	Percentage gross profit margin
Number of orders canceled	Return on investment
Volume	Customer accounts
Sales volume (by customer, product, order)	Number of new accounts
Market share	Number of accounts lost
Percentage of sales quota	Sales per new or active account
Activities	Selling expenses
Number of calls on prospects	Average cost per sales call
Number of appointments	Cost as percentage of sales volume
Number of quotations	Cost by customer type or product category

Quantitative Measures

Quantitative measures rely on straightforward, objective measures of results, such as average order value, sales volume, and number of new accounts gained. The advantage is that they are quantifiable in numbers and therefore objective. Sales managers can easily compare a salesperson's current performance with his prior one and with the current performance of colleagues. Examples of further quantitative measures are shown in Table 6.7.

Qualitative Measures

Qualitative measures can be assessed in every personal interaction. This can be done in daily business like in common meetings, phone calls, and joint customer activities. Sales managers tend to avoid using subjective criteria to evaluate salespeople's performance—as they reflect observations and opinions instead of objective facts and figures. However, qualitative measures can significantly affect a salesperson's performance and firm's reputation. Sales managers should therefore develop an evaluation system that reflects the company's objectives and encourages sales reps to perform in the desired manner. Examples of qualitative measures are shown in Table 6.8.

Only the use of both quantitative and qualitative measures enables the sales manager to see the full picture of performance and gain an holistic impression.

6.4.3   Tools for Performance Evaluation

Sales managers can use a variety of evaluation techniques. Each one has his limitations and strengths. When selecting evaluation approaches, Edwards, Cummings, and Schlacter (1984) suggest the following criteria for evaluating performance appraisal methods:

- *Job relatedness*: The method should reflect the behavior that results in performance.
- *Reliability*: The measurement should be consistent and stable over time.

Table 6.8 Qualitative measures of sales performance

Selling skills	*Self-organization*
Identification of customer needs	Planning ability
Ability to overcome price objections	Time management
Ability to close deals	Report preparation and submission
Knowledge	*Personal characteristics*
Product and service knowledge	Attitudes
Company knowledge	Initiative
Customer and market knowledge	Ethical code of conduct
Customer relationships	*Team cooperation*
Satisfaction level (e.g., service, advice)	Delivers required results
Strength of customer relations	Shares information, ideas, and credit
Reliability of the salesperson	Helps other team members

- *Validity*: The measurement should reflect what it intends to measure.
- *Standardization*: The appraisal system should be consistent throughout the company.
- *Practicality*: The method should be easy to understand, and not too costly.
- *Comparability*: The measurement should allow for easy comparison between salespeople.
- *Discriminability*: The method should distinguish among salespeople's performance.
- *Usefulness*: The appraisal system should be helpful in making decisions about, for instance, performance, promotion, training initiatives (see Sect. 6.2), and compensation.

Three major evaluating techniques that are widely used are (1) management by objectives, (2) rating scales, and (3) field accompaniments. These approaches will be outlined in the following:

1. Setting Goals—Management by Objectives

    Besides its leadership implication, MBO can be used as an efficient goal setting tool, where the sales manager and salesperson jointly agree on specific targets for the coming period—which is usually 12 months. The goals can be based on the above quantitative and qualitative measures. Because the employee should accept his targets as fair, it is usually sensible to allow them to participate in setting the goals (Hair et al., 2010).

    In some companies, salespeople must prepare a written plan for that which outlines their strategy for increasing sales with new prospects and current customers. This ensures that both agree on how goals are to be achieved. However, the establishment of the targets is ultimately the sales manager's responsibility and will inevitably be determined by overall company's objectives. When *setting sales targets*, sales managers should consider three principles:

- Goals must be *realistic* but also represent a *challenge*. Easy-to-reach goals are just as demotivating as unrealistic ones.
- Goals must be *understood* and *accepted* by the salesperson. This requires a detailed personal discussion about the path to reach these targets.
- Goals must be *achievable*. The sales manager has to provide the necessary framework for success (e.g., personnel and tangible assets).

Usually, each salesperson receives a written sales plan which will be reviewed with the manager on a regular (e.g., quarterly or monthly) basis. Continuous performance monitoring ensures that salespeople make notable progress toward their goals. It also provides guidance for altering the planned strategies and tactics to get back on track. The final step is an annual performance evaluation. Attainment of a sales target should be connected to a bonus system. The bonus can be monetary and nonmonetary. The MBO process, which is summarized in Fig. 6.12, will restart, which leads to the setting of new objectives for the coming year.

2. Rating Scales

There are several formats for the rating scale. In all cases, the sales manager must assign a salesperson a scale for various traits, skills, or sales-related results. One known way of doing this is using Likert-type scales (see Edmondson, Edwards, & Boyer, 2012 for discussion on the use of the "Likert scale"). These scales provide descriptive anchors under each segment of the scale. For example, the format of a typical five-level Likert item could be (1) unsatisfactory, (2) below average, (3) average, (4) above average, and (5) outstanding. If the sales manager must rate the sales person on the quality "needs assessment," he can then select which overall term best applies.

3. Field Accompaniments

This tool is—based on our experience—one of the most effective approaches for personal evaluation. Field accompaniments cannot only be used for training salespeople in the field as discussed in Sect. 6.2 but also for assessing qualitative measures (e.g., selling skills, knowledge). Usually, the employee schedules various appointments with customers or prospects within 1 day. The sales manager or trainer accompanies him. In between of the activities, both evaluate and analyze the conversation (e.g., emotional capability, conversation techniques, verbal and nonverbal communication). An excerpt of an evaluation sheet for conducting field accompaniments is shown in Fig. 6.13. The major advantage is that the employee receives an immediate feedback on his strengths and potentials. He can also directly put the given suggestions into practice and work on improving his selling skills in the next appointment. A major disadvantage is, however, that it is costly and time-consuming for both people.

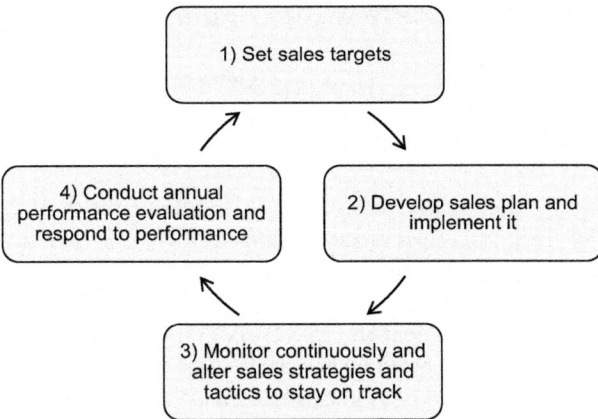

Fig. 6.12 Management by Objectives (MBO) cycle for salespeople [Source: Adapted from Hair et al. (2010, p. 446)]

Evaluation Sheet for Field Accompaniments (Excerpt)	Unsatisfactory	Below Average	Average	Above Average	Outstanding
Name: Date:					
Emotional capability					
Holding eye contact			x		
Developing emotional level (chemistry)				x	
Relaxing the conversation			x		
Conversation techniques					
Needs assessment		x			
Benefit argumentation			x		
Price talk		x			

Fig. 6.13 Evaluation sheet for field accompaniments (Excerpt)

6.4.4 Typical Errors in Performance Appraisals

Common errors and biases in appraisals (see Kahneman, 2012 for details) by sales managers, when subjectively assessing employee behavior and writing performance appraisal documents, include the following:

- *Central tendency*: Some managers often use middle-of-the-road or "play-it-safe ratings," rather than rating people at the ends of the scale. One learns very little from such ratings about true differences in performance.
- *Tendency to overrate or underrate*: Some sales leaders rate at the extremes. In this case, they are either lenient and rate every employee as good or outstanding on all rating dimensions or they are harsh and do the opposite. Again, no fundamental difference can be found which can seriously undermine the whole performance appraisal system.
- *Halo effect*: This is a common phenomenon in the use of any performance evaluation form, also in assessing and selecting new salespeople which has been discussed in Sect. 6.3.1. The halo effect appears when an overall positive or negative impression of an individual leads to rating him the same across all attributes. The overall impression dominates and leaves again little room for meaningful differentiation.
- *Recency effect*: Some sales managers have the tendency to allow more recent incidents (positive or negative) of employee behavior to carry too much weight in evaluation of performance over an entire rating period. For instance, a salesperson just acquired an important customer or a salesperson may have had a negative incident right before the performance appraisal process. Now, this is on the forefront of the manager's thoughts about that employee.
- *Similar-to-me error*: The sales manager's tendency is biased in performance evaluation toward those salespeople seen as similar to himself. For example, bias can come from attitudes and opinions about race, gender, religion, age, weight, and intelligence.

Many companies provide training and guidelines to sales managers on conducting the appraisal process and completing the forms. In order to avoid errors in performance evaluations, such forms include instructions such as:

- Read the definitions of each attribute carefully before rating
- Guard against the common tendency to overrate, to underrate, or to the middle
- Be as objective as possible. Do not let personal likes or dislikes influence your ratings
- Base your rating on the observed performance, not on potential abilities and skills
- Never rate a salesperson on one recent instance of good or poor work, but rather on general success or failure over the whole appraisal period
- Give sound reasons for your ratings. Taking notes for documentation throughout all activities helps a lot

---

How-To-Guide: Setting Goals

1) Sales manager communicates the goals of the company
2) Sales manager communicates the goals of the sales department
3) Depending on the salesperson's potential, the sales manager can choose two directions:
   - If salesperson has sales potential or positive sales attitude, the sales manager asks the sales rep to derive objectives he wants to achieve
   - If salesperson has less sales potential or negative sales attitude, the manager defines goals for the sales rep
4) Sales manager and salesperson discuss measures and activities for target achievement
5) Sales manager and salesperson make a common decision
6) Sales manager controls target achievement on a regular basis

---

Fig. 6.14 How-to guide: Setting goals

6.4.5 Conversation Techniques

Setting Goals

Management by objectives, as explained above, involves goal setting by the sales manager and salesperson. In best case, they jointly agree on the sales rep's specific goals for the coming period. The structure of a goal setting conversation is given in Fig. 6.14.

Conducting a Motivational Performance Review

Sales managers have the opportunity to meet their salespeople regularly in the field, at the office, and at sales meetings. These opportunities allow the superior to understand the personality, needs, and problems of each team member. The sales manager can out of this also better understand the individual causes of motivation (e.g., enjoying competition, incentives based on goal setting, personal appreciation) and demotivation (e.g., relationship with supervisor, personal problems, lack of advancement, lack of security, workload). As a result, he can respond in an appropriate manner that takes into account all personal and professional aspects. The structure of a motivational performance review is outlined in Fig. 6.15.

Giving Criticism—Negative Feedback

No one likes being told that part of his work is lacking, but relaying this information is a fundamental task of the sales manager's job. However, the manner in which the manager delivers criticism is absolutely important: Shouting and belittling will prevent salespeople from accepting or trusting the manager's leadership abilities. On the contrary, providing constructive criticism and support will more likely lead to respecting the manager's authority. To make the "awkward moment" a

---

How-To-Guide: Conducting a Motivational Performance Review

Phase I: "How is it currently going?"
- Sales manager listens actively; lets salesperson finish his words; takes it seriously; and observes neutrally

Phase II: "What stands in your way?"
- Salesperson lists all demotivators
- Sales manager takes everything seriously. No "It's not so bad" or "Could be worse".

Phase III: "What kind of solutions can you envision?"
- Salesperson comes up with own suggestions
- Sales manager listens actively and also provides solution approaches

Phase IV: "On what do we agree now?"
- Sales manager and salesperson make a common decision on solutions

---

Fig. 6.15 How-to guide: Conducting a motivational performance review

---

How-To-Guide: Giving Constructive Criticism

Phase I: "What are your strengths right now?"
- Sales manager listens actively; lets salesperson finish his words; and adds strengths

Phase II: "What does not work well right now?"
- Salesperson answers the question
- Sales manager gives critique by formulating his wish for the future

Phase III: "What will you do differently from now on?"
- Salesperson comes up with own suggestions as this is more motivating than receiving instructions

Phase IV: "On what do we agree now?"
- Sales manager and salesperson make a common decision on solutions

---

Fig. 6.16 How-to guide: Giving criticism—negative feedback

"productive moment," sales managers should make a fixed appointment with the employee in question and choose a private, neutral location for the meeting. A how-to guide for giving constructive critique is given in Fig. 6.16.

These three how-to guides might look at first glance too trivial for some people or too tight to conduct a natural conversation. However, experience in all industries proves that these routines are rarely used but absolutely essential to achieve ambitious results.

References

Attia, A. M., Honeycutt, E. D., Jr., & Leach, M. P. (2005). A three-stage model for assessing and improving sales force training and development. *Journal of Personal Selling and Sales Management, 25*(3), 253–268.

Bandura, A. (1986). *Social foundations of thought and action: A social cognitive theory.* Englewood Cliffs, NJ: Prentice-Hall.

Bradt, G., & Vonnegut, M. (2009). *Onboarding: How to get your new employees up to speed in half the time.* Hoboken, NJ: Wiley.

Chase, N. (1997). Raise your training ROI. *Quality, 36*, 28–41.

Dubinsky, A. J., Howell, R. D., Ingram, T. N., & Bellenger, D. N. (1986). Salesforce socialization. *Journal of Marketing, 50*, 201–203.

Edmondson, D. R., Edwards, Y. D., & Boyer, S. L. (2012). Likert scales: A marketing perspective. *International Journal of Business, Marketing, and Decision Science, 5*(2), 73–85.

Edwards, M. E., Cummings, W. T., & Schlacter, J. L. (1984). The Paris-Peoria solution: Innovations in appraising regional and international sales personnel. *Journal of Personal Selling and Sales Management, 4*(4), 26–38.

Ford, R. C., & Fottler, M. D. (1995). Empowerment: A matter of degree. *Academy of Management Executive, 9*(3), 21–29.

Francis, D., & Young, D. (2012). *Mehr Erfolg im Team. Ein Trainingsprogramm mit 46 Übungen zur Verbesserung der Leistungsfähigkeit in Arbeitsgruppen.* Hamburg: Windmühle Verlag.

Hair, J. F., Anderson, R. E., Mehta, R., & Babin, B. J. (2010). *Sales management. Building customer relationships and partnerships.* Mason, OH: South Western Cengage Learning.

Homburg, C., Schäfer, C., & Schneider, J. (2002). *Sales excellence. Vertriebsmanagement mit System* (2 Auflage). Wiesbaden: Springer Gabler.

Jobber, D., & Lancaster, G. (2012). *Selling and sales management* (9th ed.). Harlow: Pearson Education.

Johnston, M. W., & Marshall, G. W. (2013). *Sales force management. Leadership, innovation, technology* (11th ed.). New York: Routledge.

Kahneman, D. (2012). *Thinking, fast and slow.* London: Penguin Books.

Kirkpatrick, D. L. (1979). Techniques for evaluating training programs. *Training and Development Journal, 33*(6), 78–92.

Kram, K. E. (1985). *Mentoring at work: Developmental relationships in organizational life.* Lanham, MD: University Press of America.

Krishnan, B. C., Netemeyer, R. G., & Boles, J. S. (2002). Self-efficacy, competitiveness, and effort as antecedents of salesperson performance. *Journal of Personnel Selling and Sales Management, 22*(4), 285–295.

Malik, F. (2006). *Managing performing living: Effective management for a new era.* Frankfurt/Main: Campus Verlag.

Malik, F. (2010). *Management: The essence of the craft.* Frankfurt/Main: Campus Verlag.

Malik, F. (2011). *Tasks of effective management.* Frankfurt/Main: Campus Verlag.

Pettijohn, C., Pettijohn, L., & Taylor, A. J. (2007). Salesperson perceptions of ethical behaviors: Their influence on job satisfaction and turnover intentions. *Journal of Business Ethics, 78*(4), 547–557.

Schneider, B. (1987). The people make the place. *Personnel Psychology, 40*(3), 437–453.

Spitzer, D. (1995). 20 ways to motivate trainees. *Training, 32*(12), 54–57.

Tracy, B. (2010). *Goals! How to get everything you want: Faster than you ever thought possible* (2nd ed.). San Francisco: Berrett-Koehler.

Wengler, S., Ehret, M., & Saab, S. (2006). Implementation of key account management: Who, why and how? An exploratory study on the current implementation of key account management programs. *Industrial Marketing Management, 35*(1), 103–112.

Wimmer, A., Wimmer, J., Buchacher, G., & Kamp, G. (2012). *Das Beratungsgespräch: Skills und Tools für die Fachberatung.* Wien: Linde.

Yukl, G. (2006). *Leadership in organizations* (6th ed.). Upper Saddle River, NJ: Pearson Education.

Conclusion: Managing Sales Activities

7

Are you still with us? Great! Or did you just choose to read the last chapter to check whether the book contains any valuable summary and outlook? Clever approach either—because it does!

Sales is a growing but still underrated management discipline. It will be the driver of almost every successful company in the future. And it has not been described properly yet in its entirety. What has been investigated and what is the popular side of the coin is the *micro perspective*. There are plenty of "how to. . ." approaches in which salespeople find a lot of different ideas. As a side note: They are often useful but mainly stand-alone solutions. The question will always be: How do they fit into the company's business approach?

Professional sales–in the context of *the fast-moving digital age* with Big Data and amazing transparency—requires (1) a different attitude, (2) more structure, and (3) more knowledge than conventional sales. Otherwise, it will be tough to successfully differentiate.

First, it is a determined *mindset*, a convinced inner attitude, toward a clear commitment to a proactive, communicative approach, as well as a genuine interest in other people. Nothing less. If it is been seen that way, it will also be much easier integrated into so far sales-averse business areas.

Second, it is a much more *structured approach*. A clear sales process, how to proceed from customer acquisition to closing a deal and after-sales, should be a must-have for every salesperson in every ambitious company.

Third, as a consequence of this standardization, every core activity should be conducted much more regularly and more often. Through constant "learning by doing," this will lead to a significantly elevated *skill level* and therefore much better performance.

Changing perspective: What has been mainly missing so far in public as well as in literature is the—at least equivalently important—*macro approach*. This means: How to create a sales-driven (or at least: sales oriented) enterprise and free sales from the unit thinking?

© Springer International Publishing AG 2018

S. Hase, C. Busch, *The Quintessence of Sales*, Quintessence Series,

DOI 10.1007/978-3-319-61174-7_7

Because sales effects—in our *holistic understanding*— every department and every single employee. As a company, as a manager, or as a sales rep, please unleash sales out of this dogmatic restraint. Stating "the sales department is responsible for increasing market share and revenue" is a too narrow perception. It sounds strong though and may be useful for internal positioning, but it is an outdated understanding.

The new sales spirit is not meant to be carried out by only a few front liners. Up-to-date sales *involves everybody* from CEO down to the newly hired rookies. Just like in IT. This formerly "nerd department" has made its triumphal way out of the niche and now influences almost all users of all units. Today, it is crucial that everybody knows quite a bit about sales and the underlying mindset.

The macro aspect of sales is one important value driver to secure a constant business impact. An existing organizational framework elevates a "one-hit wonder" into a permanent chart-runner. The *management task* is to create this *sales-related macro framework*. This will make it possible that interfaces become more efficient and the required sales procedures do become a routine. And routine means significantly less free-styling, less trial and error, and a steeper learning curve.

Additionally, this framework will help to define the strongly required *milestones and boundaries* for sales leadership, training, recruiting, and evaluation.

This approach in total might probably bring some chances for quite a large number of employees. Managing sales activities is therefore also to a certain part *change management*. As discussed by Duhigg (2012) in his interesting approach, it should be some efforts worth to understand "the power of habit" and "why we do what we do and how to change" as well as to understand the golden rules of habit change.

One more thing: The practical handling of the interdependencies of *sales and ethics* will be a growing topic in future. The task is to stand the temptation and not to misuse ethics as a marketing tool, but genuinely act accordingly to it in daily business.

We hope you have enjoyed reading this book and found it useful. We assure you that if you put all of this together, you will be successful in boosting your business. Because this is exactly what we are doing since 2004. And the good news is: It works. No matter what your position and your background is—in the end everyone sells something at some points in life. Enjoy the journey and the development.

Good luck in your sales career!

Stefan and Corinna

Phone: +49 (0) 40 235 13 08-0

Email: quintessence@wirkungplus.de

Webpage: wirkungplus.de/en

Reference

Duhigg, C. (2012). *The power of habit. Why we do what we do and how to change.* London: William Heinemann.

About the Authors

Stefan Hase studied business administration in Hamburg and began his career in sales in 1993 at Konica Business Machines. In 1997, he moved to Triumph-Adler, where he became human resource manager. He was there responsible for the operative personnel development of 2500 employees and the transformation of the company into a sales driven enterprise. On the basis of his rich experience, he founded Wirkung Plus in 2004. The subsidiary Eins Plus—Deutsche Vertriebsakademie followed in 2008. Stefan Hase works as business consultant, trainer, and keynote speaker for many well-known customers—such as Hewlett-Packard, DNV GL, Samsung, and Sennheiser—both on strategic and operational level.

Over the last decade he has designed and conducted numerous sales programs in Europe, Asia, North and South America, and trained hundreds of employees in the above-named markets. Besides his highly appreciated classroom sessions, he is also very successful in the field of coaching sales managers in their daily business. His accompaniments of relevant projects in markets such as Brazil, China or USA has provided him with a vast experience from eastern to western sales styles. He is one of the few globally experienced sales specialists.

Email: s.hase@wirkungplus.de

© Springer International Publishing AG 2018   127
S. Hase, C. Busch, *The Quintessence of Sales*, Quintessence Series,
DOI 10.1007/978-3-319-61174-7

Corinna Busch completed her vocational training as a shipping management assistant and received a B.A. in Logistics Management from Hamburg School of Business Administration (HSBA). After three years of working in sales and customer service positions, she studied Organizational Behaviour (M.Sc) at Aston Business School, UK. She studied, among others, the behavior of employees, teams and organizations in the implementation of strategic decisions. She came to Wirkung Plus in April 2012. As sales coach and consultant, she advises, trains and coaches employees from various industries along the sales process. At Eins Plus—Deutsche Vertriebsakademie, she is also responsible for the sales training of students who are enrolled in the FIBAA accredited distance-learning degree course "Sales & Management (B.A.)". This training program takes place in cooperation with the Euro-FH in Hamburg (University of Applied Sciences).

Email: c.busch@wirkungplus.de

References

Anderson, R. E., Dubinsky, A. J., & Mehta, R. (1999). Sales managers: Marketing's best example of the peter principle? *Business Horizons, 42*(1), 19–26.

Attia, A. M., Honeycutt, E. D., Jr., & Leach, M. P. (2005). A three-stage model for assessing and improving sales force training and development. *Journal of Personal Selling and Sales Management, 25*(3), 253–268.

Babin, B. J., Boles, J. S., & Robin, D. P. (2000). Representing the perceived ethical work climate among marketing employees. *Journal of the Academy of Marketing Science, 28*(3), 345–358.

Bandura, A. (1986). *Social foundations of thought and action: A social cognitive theory.* Englewood Cliffs, NJ: Prentice-Hall.

Biemans, W. G., Brenčič, M. M., & Malshe, A. (2010). Marketing-sales interface configurations in B2B firms. *Industrial Marketing Management, 39*(2), 183–194.

Bradt, G., & Vonnegut, M. (2009). *Onboarding: How to get your new employees up to speed in half the time.* Hoboken, NJ: Wiley.

Brown, M. E., Treviño, L. K., & Harrison, D. A. (2005). Ethical leadership: A social learning perspective for construct development and testing. *Organizational Behavior and Human Decision Processes, 97*(2), 117–134.

Cadogan, J. W., Lee, N., Tarkiainen, A., & Sundqvist, S. (2009). Sales manager and sales team determinants of salesperson ethical behavior. *European Journal of Marketing, 43*(7/8), 907–937.

Chase, N. (1997). Raise your training ROI. *Quality, 36*, 28–41.

Dabholkar, P. A., & Kellaris, J. J. (1992). Toward understanding marketing students' ethical judgment of controversial personal selling practices. *Journal of Business Research, 24*(4), 313–329.

De Gennaro, A. (2015). Post-closing issues deserve attention to avoid optical buyer's remorse. *Ophthalmology Times, 40*(7), 69–70.

DeCarlo, T. E., & Lam, S. K. (2016). Identifying effective hunters and farmers in the salesforce: A dispositional-situational framework. *Journal of the Academy of Marketing Science, 44*(4), 415–439.

DeCormier, R. A., & Jobber, D. (1993). The counselor selling method. Concepts and constructs. *Journal of Personal Selling and Sales Management, 23*(4), 39–59.

Deeter-Schmelz, D. R., Goebel, D. J., & Kennedy, K. N. (2008). What are the characteristics of an effective sales manager? An exploratory study comparing salesperson and sales manager perspectives. *Journal of Personnel Selling and Sales Management, 28*(1), 7–20.

Dewsnap, B., & Jobber, D. (2000). The sales-marketing interface in consumer packaged goods companies: A conceptual framework. *Journal of Personal Selling and Sales Management, 20*(2), 109–119.

Dickson, M. W., Smith, D. B., Grojean, M. W., & Ehrhart, M. (2001). An organizational climate regarding ethics: The outcome of leader values and the practices that reflect them. *The Leadership Quarterly, 12*(2), 197–217.

© Springer International Publishing AG 2018   129
S. Hase, C. Busch, *The Quintessence of Sales*, Quintessence Series,
DOI 10.1007/978-3-319-61174-7

Doran, G. T. (1981). There's a S.M.A.R.T. way to write management's goals and objectives. *Management Review, 70*(11), 35–36.

Dubinsky, A. J., Howell, R. D., Ingram, T. N., & Bellenger, D. N. (1986). Salesforce socialization. *Journal of Marketing, 50*, 201–203.

Duhigg, C. (2012). *The power of habit. Why we do what we do and how to change.* London: William Heinemann.

Edmondson, D. R., Edwards, Y. D., & Boyer, S. L. (2012). Likert scales: A marketing perspective. *International Journal of Business, Marketing, and Decision Science, 5*(2), 73–85.

Edwards, M. E., Cummings, W. T., & Schlacter, J. L. (1984). The Paris-Peoria solution: Innovations in appraising regional and international sales personnel. *Journal of Personal Selling and Sales Management, 4*(4), 26–38.

Ford, R. C., & Fottler, M. D. (1995). Empowerment: A matter of degree. *Academy of Management Executive, 9*(3), 21–29.

Francis, D., & Young, D. (2012). *Mehr Erfolg im Team. Ein Trainingsprogramm mit 46 Übungen zur Verbesserung der Leistungsfähigkeit in Arbeitsgruppen.* Hamburg: Windmühle Verlag.

Guenzi, P., & Troilo, G. (2007). The joint contribution of marketing and sales to the creation of superior customer value. *Journal of Business Research, 60*(2), 98–107.

Hair, J. F., Anderson, R. E., Mehta, R., & Babin, B. J. (2010). *Sales management. Building customer relationships and partnerships.* Mason, OH: South Western Cengage Learning.

Homburg, C., Schäfer, C., & Schneider, J. (2002). *Sales Excellence. Vertriebsmanagement mit System* (2 Auflage). Wiesbaden: Springer Gabler.

Jobber, D., & Lancaster, G. (2012). *Selling and sales management* (9th ed.). Harlow: Pearson Education.

Johnston, M. W., & Marshall, G. W. (2013). *Sales force management. Leadership, innovation, technology* (11th ed.). New York: Routledge.

Kahneman, D. (2012). *Thinking, fast and slow.* London: Penguin Books.

Kirkpatrick, D. L. (1979). Techniques for evaluating training programs. *Training and Development Journal, 33*(6), 78–92.

Kram, K. E. (1985). *Mentoring at work: Developmental relationships in organizational life.* Lanham, MD: University Press of America.

Kreutzer, R., Rumler, A., & Wille-Baumkauff, B. (2014). *B2B-Online-Marketing und Social Media. Ein Praxisleitfaden.* Wiesbaden, Springer Gabler.

Krishnan, B. C., Netemeyer, R. G., & Boles, J. S. (2002). Self-efficacy, competitiveness, and effort as antecedents of salesperson performance. *Journal of Personnel Selling and Sales Management, 22*(4), 285–295.

MacInnis, D. J., & Jaworski, B. J. (1989). Information processing from advertisements: Toward an integrative framework. *Journal of Marketing, 53*, 1–23.

Malik, F. (2006). *Managing performing living: Effective management for a new era.* Frankfurt/Main: Campus Verlag.

Malik, F. (2010). *Management: The essence of the craft.* Frankfurt/Main: Campus Verlag.

Malik, F. (2011). *Tasks of effective management.* Frankfurt/Main: Campus Verlag.

Marshall, G. W., Goebel, D. J., & Moncrief, W. C. (2003). Hiring for success at the buyer-seller interface. *Journal of Business Research, 56*(4), 247–255.

McBane, D. (1995). Empathy and the salesperson: A multidimenional perspective. *Psychology and Marketing, 12*(4), 349–371.

Moncrief, W. C., & Marshall, G. W. (2005). The evolution of the seven steps of selling. *Industrial Marketing Management, 34*(1), 13–22.

Mulki, J. P., Jaramillo, J. F., & Locander, W. B. (2009). Critical role of leadership on ethical climate and salesperson behaviors. *Journal of Business Ethics, 86*, 125–141.

Pettijohn, C., Pettijohn, L., & Taylor, A. J. (2007). Salesperson perceptions of ethical behaviors: Their influence on job satisfaction and turnover intentions. *Journal of Business Ethics, 78*(4), 547–557.

Pilling, B. K., & Eroglu, S. (1994). An empirical examination of the impact of salesperson empathy and professionalism and salability on retail buyers' evaluations. *Journal of Personal Selling and Sales Management, 14*(1), 55–58.

Rackham, N. (1988). *SPIN selling*. New York: McGraw-Hill.

Rozell, E. J., Pettijohn, C. E., & Parker, R. S. (2006). Emotional intelligence and dispositional affectivity as predictors of performance in salespeople. *Journal of Marketing Theory and Practice, 14*(2), 113–124.

Schneider, B. (1987). The people make the place. *Personnel Psychology, 40*(3), 437–453.

Schweitzer, M. E., Ordóñez, L., & Douma, B. (2004). Goal setting as a motivator of unethical behavior. *Academy of Management Journal, 47*(3), 422–432.

Schwepker, C. H., & Good, D. J. (2004). Marketing control and sales force customer orientation. *Journal of Personal Selling and Sales Management, 24*(3), 167–179.

Schwepker, C. H., & Hartline, M. D. (2005). Managing the ethical climate of customer-contact service employees. *Journal of Service Research, 7*(4), 377–397.

Smith, T. M., Gopalakrishna, S., & Chatterjee, R. (2006). A three-stage model of integrated marketing communications. *Journal of Marketing Research, 43*(4), 564–579.

Spitzer, D. (1995). 20 ways to motivate trainees. *Training, 32*(12), 54–57.

Strout, E. (2002). To tell the truth. *Sales and Marketing Management, 154*(7), 40–47.

Tracy, B. (2010). *Goals! How to get everything you want: Faster than you ever thought possible* (2nd ed.). San Francisco, CA: Berrett-Koehler.

Tracy, B. (2015). *Sales management*. New York: American Management Association.

Tschohl, J. (2008). *Achieving excellence through customer service* (5th ed.). Minneapolis, MN: Best Sellers Publishing.

Turner, J., & Shah, R. (2010). *The top 10 things you must know about measuring ROI on social media marketing*. Upper Saddle River, NJ: Pearson Education.

Weitz, B. A., & Bradford, K. D. (1999). Personal selling and sales management: A relationship marketing perspective. *Academy of Marketing Science, 27*(2), 241–254.

WeltN24. (2013). Mit diesem Team formt Guardiola die neuen Bayern [online]. Accessed January 10, 2017, from https://www.welt.de/sport/fussball/bundesliga/fc-bayern-muenchen/arti cle117291152/Mit-diesem-Team-formt-Guardiola-die-neuen-Bayern.html

Wengler, S., Ehret, M., & Saab, S. (2006). Implementation of key account management: Who, why and how? An exploratory study on the current implementation of key account management programs. *Industrial Marketing Management, 35*(1), 103–112.

Wimmer, A., Wimmer, J., Buchacher, G., & Kamp, G. (2012). *Das Beratungsgespräch: Skills und Tools für die Fachberatung*. Wien: Linde.

Yukl, G. (2006). *Leadership in organizations* (6th ed.). Upper Saddle River, NJ: Pearson Education.

Ziglar, Z. (2003). *Ziglar on selling. The ultimate handbook for the complete sales profession*. Nashville: Thomas Nelson.

Printed by Printforce, the Netherlands